THE COMIC

THE COMIC SPIRIT

JOSEPH F. LITTELL

EDITOR

JOY LITTELL

CONSULTANT ON TEXT
AND ILLUSTRATIONS

REVISED EDITION

LOTHROP, LEE & SHEPARD COMPANY/1975

A DIVISION OF WILLIAM MORROW & COMPANY
NEW YORK

Design **William A. Seabright**

Acknowledgments: See page 158

Printed in the United States of America.

1 2 3 4 5 79 78 77 76 75

Library of Congress Catalog Card
Number 75−7681

ISBN 0−688-41720-5
ISBN 0−688-51720-X

CONTENTS

WILD LIFE

Ogden Nash

THE TURTLE

The turtle lives 'twixt plated decks
Which practically conceal its sex.
I think it clever of the turtle
In such a fix to be so fertile.

THE FISH

The fish, when he's exposed to air,
Can show no trace of savoir faire,
But in the sea regains his balance
And exploits all his manly talents.
The chastest of the vertebrates,
He never even sees his mates,
But when they've finished, he appears
And O.K.'s all their bright ideas.

THE RABBITS

Here's a verse about rabbits
That doesn't mention their habits.

THE COW

The cow is of the bovine ilk;
One end is moo, the other, milk.

THE PIGEON

There is nothing in any religion
Which compels us to love the pigeon.

THE SHREW

Strange as it seems, the smallest mammal
Is the shrew, and not the camel.
And that is all I ever knew,
Or wish to know, about the shrew.

THE RHINOCEROS

The rhino is a homely beast,
For human eyes he's not a feast.
Farewell, farewell, you old rhinoceros,
I'll stare at something less prepoceros.

THE GERM

A mighty creature is the germ,
Though smaller than the pachyderm.
His customary dwelling place
Is deep within the human race.
His childish pride he often pleases
By giving people strange diseases.
Do you, my poppet, feel infirm?
You probably contain a germ.

A New Natural History

James Thurber

The Common Carrier.

The male and female Tryst.

A female Volt
with all her Ergs
in one Gasket.

The female Snarl (left)
and the male Sulk.

An Upstart rising from a clump of Johnny-Come-Lately.
The small rodent (right) is a Spouse.

The male Wedlock (left)
cautiously approaching a clump
of Devil-May-Care;
at right, the female.

A female Shriek (right) rising out of the Verbiage
to attack a female Swoon.

Two widely distributed rodents:
the Barefaced Lie (left)
and the White Lie.

The Early and the Late Riser.

The Living, or Spitting, Image (left)
and a Dead Ringer.

The Troth, Plighted (right)
and Unplighted.

A TRIO OF PREHISTORIC CREATURES

Left to right: the Thesaurus, the Stereopticon, and the Hexameter.
The tree is a Sacroiliac.

The Hopeless Quandary.

SLEEPING ARRANGEMENTS

Sam Levenson

"It is not good for man to be alone," Papa used to say, quoting from the *Poor Man's Almanac of Rationalizations*—so we slept in various sets: four in a bed (the group plan); three in a bed (semiprivate, unless one of the three had a contagious disease, in which case he was allowed to sleep with only one, preferably one who had never had the disease); two in a bed (doubleheader); and one in a bed (critical list). Hopeless cases slept in Mama's bed. Chairs and floors also served as beds. Floors were preferred because you could not fall off.

In order to insure a reasonable amount of air not already filtered through our bed partner's adenoids, we slept not tête-à-tête but foot-à-tête—cross-ventilation we called it—an arrangement that made it impossible to cough into a brother's face; we could cough only into his feet.

There were other sleeping patterns such as crisscross, ticktacktoe, checkerboard, pyramids and shambles. A sudden sneeze by the kid in the middle of any of these configurations could trigger a chain reaction which sent kids flying in all directions.

The procedure of getting bedded down for the night often started with the shock treatment. Just before bedtime Mama would reel in the clothesline, remove several sheets of ice which earlier in the day had been sheets of linen, put them on your bed and say, "Go to bed." Those were the nights when nobody fought to be first in bed. Mama would reduce the intensity of the shock by placing a hot stove lid wrapped in a towel at your feet. I still carry the name of the stove manufacturer branded on my left arch.

Some people brag that they sleep like a rock. I slept *on* one. Mama's pillows were about the size of a home movie screen and were as hard as bags of cement. You slept with your head propped up as though you were lying in state. Years later, as we got married, Mama made each of us a present of a set of pillows extracted from the mother pillow. Still, no matter how much stuffing Mama pulled out of the original, it never got softer.

For most people, sound sleep implies quiet. We slept through the sounds of a world that never slept. Our nervous systems were geared to noise. Silence would have shocked us. We slept through the din of fire engines, trolleys, trucks, trains, slamming doors, barking dogs and wailing cats. Within our own walls plumbing hummed, faucets chirped, bedsprings twanged, stoves hissed, mattresses groaned, floors creaked, windows banged, and the window shades wildly applauded all the performances.

While there was room for all to sleep, quilts were at a premium, as were brothers with warm feet. The latter sold high on the open market. Deals for quilts were made before bedtime. We called it the Cover Charge. "Hey, Al! If you let me have the heavy quilt tonight I'll give you my searchlight for lend for two days." The heavy quilt was not warm, just heavy, but therein lay its merit. It didn't slide off the bed. It rested there like a mound of earth on a fresh grave, and we slept the sleep of the just. That quilt could cover three of us, if one of us were not my brother Mike, who was not just a restless sleeper—he was a night crawler. He would start moving across the bed on a forty-five degree angle from the footboard to the headboard, instinctively dragging the quilt along his route. We held on for dear life and he dragged us, quilt and all, wherever he was going. The tug-of-war lasted until we all fell asleep from sheer exhaustion.

Papa's heavy coat was a prize. He had brought it from the old, cold country and it was lined with fur. We could slip our feet through the sleeves, button ourselves into the hairy straitjacket and hibernate for one winter's night at a time.

The coldest room in the house was the front room. To get any warmth into it you would have had to open the windows. Mama used to keep her marinated fish there. In order to survive the night in that room you wore a sweater under your nightshirt, and long woolen socks. But Mother Nature, not nearly so kind as our own mother, had a way of taunting us on extra-cold nights. Just when you were nice and warm, the call came. You tried to throw her off your track by concentrating on deserts, droughts, sand dunes or petrified forests—all to no avail.

"Hey, Al. Come with me. It's dark." It was not the dark alone I was afraid of. There was the ghoulish red face of the hot coal stove and, even more frightening, the phosphorescent glow of Mama's teeth in a glass in the kitchen.

Al wouldn't come. "Not me, buddy."

"I'll give you my searchlight for lend for *three* days."

"Make it a week."

"O.K. If you throw in the heavy quilt."

"It's a deal."

Together we made the trip to the toilet, dragging the bartered quilt after us lest some older brother roll up in it and claim seniority rights.

JABBERWOCKY

Lewis Carroll

'Twas brillig, and the slithy toves
   Did gyre and gimble in the wabe:
All mimsy were the borogoves,
   And the mome raths outgrabe.

"Beware the Jabberwock, my son!
   The jaws that bite, the claws that catch!
Beware the Jubjub bird, and shun
   The frumious Bandersnatch!"

He took his vorpal sword in hand:
   Long time the manxome foe he sought—
So rested he by the Tumtum tree,
   And stood awhile in thought.

And, as in uffish thought he stood,
   The Jabberwock, with eyes of flame,
Came whiffling through the tulgey wood,
   And burbled as it came!

One, two! One, two! And through and through
   The vorpal blade went snicker-snack!
He left it dead, and with its head
   He went galumphing back.

"And hast thou slain the Jabberwock?
   Come to my arms, my beamish boy!
O frabjous day! Callooh! Callay!"
   He chortled in his joy.

'Twas brillig, and the slithy toves
   Did gyre and gimble in the wabe:
All mimsy were the borogoves,
   And the mome raths outgrabe.

JABBER-WHACKY

or on Dreaming after Falling Asleep Watching TV

Isabelle Di Caprio

'Twas Brillo, and the G.E. Stoves,
  Did Procter-Gamble in the Glade;
All Pillsbury were the Taystee loaves,
  And in a Minute Maid.

"Beware the Station-Break, my son!
  The voice that lulls, the ads that vex!
Beware the Doctors Claim, and shun
  That horror called Brand-X!"

He took his Q-Tip'd swab in hand;
  Long time the Tension Headache fought—
So Dristan he by a Mercury,
  And Bayer-break'd in thought.

And as in Bufferin Gulf he stood,
  The Station-Break, with Rise of Tame,
Came Wisking through the Pride-hazed wood,
  And Creme-Rinsed as it came!

Buy one! Buy two! We're almost through!
  The Q-Tip'd Dash went Spic and Span!
He Tide Air-Wick, and with Bisquick
  Went Aero-Waxing Ban.

"And has thou Dreft the Station-Break?
  Ajax the Breck, Excedrin boy!
Oh, Fab wash day, Cashmere Bouquet!"
  He Handi-Wrapped with Joy.

'Twas Brillo, and the G.E. Stoves,
  Did Procter-Gamble in the Glade;
All Pillsbury were the Taystee loaves,
  And in a Minute Maid.

PLANE GEOMETRY

Emma Round

'Twas Euclid, and the theorem pi
   Did plane and solid in the text,
All parallel were the radii,
   And the ang-gulls convex'd.

"Beware the Wentworth-Smith, my son,
   And the Loci that vacillate;
Beware the Axiom, and shun
   The faithless Postulate."

He took his Waterman in hand;
   Long time the proper proof he sought;
Then rested he by the XYZ
   And sat awhile in thought.

And as in inverse thought he sat
   A brilliant proof, in lines of flame,
All neat and trim, it came to him,
   Tangenting as it came.

"AB, CD," reflected he—
   The Waterman went snicker-snack—
He Q.E.D.-ed, and, proud indeed,
   He trapezoided back.

"And hast thou proved the 29th?
   Come to my arms, my radius boy!
O good for you! O one point two!"
   He rhombused in his joy.

'Twas Euclid, and the theorem pi
   Did plane and solid in the text;
All parallel were the radii,
   And the ang-gulls convex'd.

CHRISTMAS AFTERNOON

(Done in the Manner,
if Not the Spirit,
of Dickens)

Robert C. Benchley

What an afternoon! Mr. Gummidge said that, in his estimation, there never had *been* such an afternoon since the world began, a sentiment which was heartily endorsed by Mrs. Gummidge and all the little Gummidges, not to mention the relatives who had come over from Jersey for the day.

In the first place, there was the *ennui*. And such *ennui* as it was! A heavy, overpowering *ennui*, such as results from a participation in eight courses of steaming, gravied food, topping off with salted nuts which the little old spinster Gummidge from Oak Hill said she never knew when to stop eating—and true enough she didn't—a dragging, devitalizing *ennui*, which left its victims strewn about the living-room in various attitudes of prostration suggestive of those of the petrified occupants in a newly un-earthed Pompeiian dwelling; an *ennui* which carried with it a retinue of yawns, snarls and thinly veiled insults, and which ended in ruptures in the clan spirit serious enough to last throughout the glad new year.

Then there were the toys! Three and a quarter dozen toys to be divid-ed among seven children. Surely enough, you or I might say, to satisfy the little tots. But that would be because we didn't know the tots. In came Baby Lester Gummidge, Lillian's boy, dragging an electric grain-elevator which happened to be the only toy in the entire collection which ap-pealed to little Norman, five-year-old son of Luther, who lived in Rahway. In came curly-headed Effie in frantic and throaty disputation with Arthur, Jr., over the possession of an articulated zebra. In came Everett, bearing a mechanical Negro which would no longer dance, owing to a previous forcible feeding by the baby of a marshmallow into its only available aperture. In came Fonlansbee, teeth buried in the hand of little Ormond, which bore a popular but battered remnant of what had once been the proud false-bosom of a hussar's uniform. In they all came, one after another, some crying, some snapping, some pulling, some pushing—all appealing to their respective parents for aid in their intramural warfare.

And the cigar smoke! Mrs. Gummidge said that she didn't mind the smoke from a good cigarette, but would they mind if she opened the windows for just a minute in order to clear the room of the heavy aroma of used cigars? Mr. Gummidge stoutly maintained that they were good cigars. His brother, George Gummidge, said that he, likewise, would say that they were. At which colloquial sally both the Gummidge brothers laughed testily, thereby breaking the laughter record for the afternoon.

Aunt Libbie, who lived with George, remarked from the dark corner of the room that it seemed just like Sunday to her. An amendment was offered to this statement by the cousin, who was in the insurance business, stating that it was worse than Sunday. Murmurings indicative of as hearty agreement with this sentiment as their lethargy would allow came from the other members of the family circle, causing Mr. Gummidge to suggest a walk in the air to settle their dinner.

And then arose such a chorus of protestations as has seldom been heard. It was too cloudy to walk. It was too raw. It looked like snow. It looked like rain. Luther Gummidge said that he must be starting along home soon, anyway, bringing forth the acid query from Mrs. Gummidge as to whether or not he was bored. Lillian said that she felt a cold coming on, and added that something they had had for dinner must have been undercooked. And so it went, back and forth, forth and back, up and down, and in and out, until Mr. Gummidge's suggestion of a walk in the air was reduced to a tattered impossibility and the entire company glowed with ill-feeling.

In the meantime, we must not forget the children. No one else could. Aunt Libbie said that she didn't think there was anything like children to make a Christmas; to which Uncle Ray, the one with the Masonic fob, said, "No, thank God!" Although Christmas is supposed to be the season of good cheer, you (or I, for that matter) couldn't have told, from listening to the little ones, but what it was the children's Armageddon season, when Nature had decreed that only the fittest should survive, in order that the race might be carried on by the strongest, the most predatory and those possessing the best protective coloring. Although there were constant admonitions to Fonlansbee to "Let Ormond have that now; it's his," and to Arthur, Jr., not to be selfish, but to "give the kiddie-car to Effie; she's smaller than you are," the net result was always that Fonlansbee kept the whistle and Arthur, Jr., rode in permanent, albeit disputed, possession of the kiddie-car. Oh, that we mortals should set ourselves up against the inscrutable workings of Nature!

Hallo! A great deal of commotion! That was Uncle George stumbling over the electric train, which had early in the afternoon ceased to function and which had been left directly across the threshold. A great deal of crying! That was Arthur, Jr., bewailing the destruction of his already useless train, about which he had forgotten until the present moment. A great deal of recrimination! That was Arthur, Sr., and George fixing it up. And finally a great crashing! That was Baby Lester pulling over the tree on top of himself, necessitating the bringing to bear of all of Uncle Ray's knowledge of forestry to extricate him from the wreckage.

And finally Mrs. Gummidge passed the Christmas candy around. Mr. Gummidge afterward admitted that this was a tactical error on the part of his spouse. I no more believe that Mrs. Gummidge thought they wanted that Christmas candy than I believe that she thought they wanted the cold turkey which she later suggested. My opinion is that she wanted to drive them home. At any rate, that is what she succeeded in doing. Such cries as there were of "Ugh! Don't let me see another thing to eat!" and "Take it away!" Then came hurried scramblings in the coat-closet for overshoes. There were the rasping sounds made by cross parents when putting wraps on children. There were insincere exhortations to "come and see us soon" and to "get together for lunch some time." And, finally, there were slammings of doors and the silence of utter exhaustion, while Mrs. Gummidge went about picking up stray sheets of wrapping paper.

And, as Tiny Tim might say in speaking of Christmas afternoons as an institution, "God help us, every one."

HAPPY CHILDHOOD TALES

Robert C. Benchley

We have had so many stories lately dealing with the sordid facts of life, about kitchen sinks and lynchings and young girls thrown out into the streets by mean old farmers who live in horsehair trunks, to say nothing of incidental subjects, such as gin and cold oatmeal and unfortunate people who have only one glove apiece, that a reaction is taking place in the mind of the reading public and a demand is going up for some of the fanciful happy tales of our youth.

"Enough of these stories of crime and unhappiness!" the people are crying. "Tell us again some of the ancient myths of an older day, the gay little legends on which we were brought up before the world grew grim and sordid."

And so, my little readers, I am going to try to recall to you some of the charming fairy tales, or, at any rate, to make up some like them, and I hope that after this little trip back into the Never-Never Land of our youth, those little cheeks of yours will be blooming again and that you will shut your traps. For, after all, there must be *some* good in the world, else why were erasers put on the ends of lead pencils?

ENDREMIA AND LIASON

(From the Greek Mythology)

ndremia was the daughter of Polygaminous, the God of Ensilage, and Reba, the Goddess of Licorice. She was the child of a most unhappy union, it later turned out, for when she was a tiny child her father struck her mother with an anvil and turned himself into a lily pad to avoid the vengeance of Jove. But Jove was too sly for Polygaminous and struck him with a bolt of lightning the size of the Merchants Bank Building which threw him completely off his balance so that he toppled over into a chasm and was dashed to death.

In the meantime, Little Endremia found herself alone in the world with nobody but Endocrine, the Goddess of Lettuce, and her son Bilax, the God of Gum Arabic, to look after her. But, as Polygaminous (her father; have you forgotten so soon, you dope?) had turned Endremia into a mushroom before he turned himself into a lily pad, neither of her guardians knew who she was, so their protection did her no good.

But Jove had not so soon forgotten the daughter of his favorite (Reba), and appeared to her one night in the shape of a mushroom gatherer. He asked her how she would like to get off that tree (she was one of those mushrooms which grow on trees) and get into his basket. Endremia, not knowing that it was Jove who was asking her, said not much. Whereupon Jove unloosed his mighty wrath and struck down the whole tree with a bolt of lightning which he had brought with him in case Endremia wouldn't listen to reason.

This is why it is never safe to eat the mushrooms which grow on trees, or to refuse to get into Jove's basket.

MILGRIG AND THE THREE WILFS

(Something like Hans Christian Andersen)

nce upon a time there was a little girl named Milgrig, believe it or not. She lived in the middle of a deep dark forest with her three ugly sisters and their husbands, who were charcoal burners. Every night the three ugly sisters used to take little Milgrig and pull out a strand of her golden hair, so that by the time she was thirteen years old she looked something awful. And after the three sisters had pulled out her hair, their three husbands (I forgot to tell you that the three husbands were even uglier than the three sisters and much nastier) would stick pins into little Milgrig until she looked like a war map.

One night, when little Milgrig was so full of pins that she couldn't see straight, a fairy prince came riding up to the door of the charcoal burners' hut and asked if he had lost his way.

"How should I know?" replied the oldest sister, who was uglier than all the rest. "What was your way?"

"My way was to the king's castle," replied the prince, "and I must get there before midnight, for my father is torturing my mother with red-hot irons."

"Your father sounds like a good egg," replied the oldest husband, who was uglier than all the rest. "We must ask him down some night."

The prince, however, did not think that this was very funny and asked if little Milgrig might not be allowed to show him the way to the castle.

The ugly husbands and sisters, thinking that Milgrig would not know the way and would get the prince lost in the forest, agreed heartily to this suggestion, and the pins were pulled out of Milgrig to make it possible for her to walk.

"Good luck and a happy landing!" they all called out after the two young people as they set forth on their perilous journey.

But the prince was no fool, and knew his way through the forest as well as you or I do (better, I'll wager), and he took little Milgrig to the palace just as fast as his palfrey would carry him.

She wasn't particularly crazy about going, but a prince is a prince, and she knew enough to keep her mouth shut.

When they reached the palace and the prince found that his father had already killed his mother, he turned to little Milgrig and said:

"Now you are the queen."

At this, little Milgrig was very pleased and immediately dispatched messengers to the charcoal burners' hut, where the three ugly sisters and three still uglier brothers-in-law were burned alive in a slow fire. Little Milgrig and the prince, happy in this termination to their little affair, lived happily ever after.

AT THE FUNERAL

Mark Twain

Do not criticize the person in whose honor the entertainment is given.

Make no remarks about his equipment. If the handles are plated, it is best to seem to not observe it.

If the odor of the flowers is too oppressive for your comfort, remember that they were not brought there for you, and that the person for whom they were brought suffers no inconvenience from their presence.

Listen, with as intense an expression of attention as you can command, to the official statement of the character and history of the person in whose honor the entertainment is given; and if these statistics should seem to fail to tally with the facts, in places, do not nudge your neighbor, or press your foot upon his toes, or manifest, by any other sign, your awareness that taffy is being distributed.

If the official hopes expressed concerning the person in whose honor the entertainment is given are known by you to be oversized, let it pass— do not interrupt.

At the moving passages, be moved—but only according to the degree of your intimacy with the parties giving the entertainment, or with the party in whose honor the entertainment is given. Where a blood relation sobs, an intimate friend should choke up, a distant acquaintance should sigh, a stranger should merely fumble sympathetically with his handkerchief. Where the occasion is military, the emotions should be graded according to military rank, the highest officer present taking precedence in emotional violence, and the rest modifying their feelings according to their position in the service.

Do not bring your dog.

AT A FIRE

Mark Twain

Form of Tender of Rescue from Strange Young Gentleman to Strange Young Lady at a Fire.

> Although through the fiat of a cruel fate, I have been debarred the gracious privilege of your acquaintance, permit me, Miss [here insert name, if known], the inestimable honor of offering you the aid of a true and loyal arm against the fiery doom which now o'ershadows you with its crimson wing. [This form to be memorized, and practiced in private.]

Should she accept, the young gentleman should offer his arm—bowing, and observing "Permit me"—and so escort her to the fire escape and deposit her in it (being extremely careful, if she have no clothes on but her night dress, not to seem to notice the irregularity). No form of leave-taking is permissible, further than a formal bow, accompanied by a barely perceptible smile of deferential gratitude for the favor which the young lady has accorded—this smile to be completed at the moment the fire escape starts to slide down, then the features to be recomposed instantly.

A compulsory introduction at a fire is not binding upon the young lady. The young gentleman cannot require recognition at her hands when he next meets her, but must leave her unembarrassed to decide for herself whether she will continue the acquaintanceship or ignore it.

To return to the fire. If the boarding house is not provided with a fire escape, the young gentleman will use such other means of rescue as circumstances shall afford. But he will not need to change the form of his proffer of assistance; for this speech has been purposely framed in such a way as to apply with equal felicity to all methods of rescue from fire. If egress may be had to the street by the stairway, the young gentleman will offer his arm and escort the young lady down; if retreat in that direction is cut off by the fire, he will escort her to the floor above and lower her to the street by a rope, fastening it by slip-noose under her armpits, with the knot behind (at the same time bowing and saying "Permit me"); or if no rope be procurable, he will drop her from the balcony upon soft substances to be provided by the populace below—always observing "Permit me," and accompanying the remark with a slight inclination of the head. In either ascending or descending the stairs, the young gentleman shall walk beside the young lady, if the stairs are wide enough to allow it; otherwise he must *precede* her. In no case must he follow her. This is *de rigueur*.

In rescuing a chambermaid, presentation of card is not necessary, neither should one say "Permit me." The form of tender service should also be changed. Example:

Form of Tender of Rescue from Young Gentleman to Chambermaid at a Fire.

There is no occasion for alarm, Mary [insertion of surname not permissible]; keep cool, do everything just as I tell you, and, *D.V.,* I will save you.

Anything more elaborate than this, as to diction and sentiment, would be in exceedingly bad taste, in the case of a chambermaid. Yet at the same time, brusqueries are to be avoided. Such expressions as "Come, git!" should never fall from the lips of a true gentleman at a fire. No, not even when addressed to the humblest domestic. Brevity is well; but even brevity cannot justify vulgarity.

In assisting at a fire in a boarding house, the true gentleman will always save the young ladies first—making no distinction in favor of personal attractions, or social eminence, or pecuniary predominance—but taking them as they come, and firing them out with as much celerity as shall be consistent with decorum. There are exceptions, of course, to all rules; the exceptions to this one are:

Partiality, in the matter of rescue, to be shown to:

1 Fiancées
2 Persons toward whom the operator feels a tender sentiment, but has not yet declared himself
3 Sisters
4 Stepsisters
5 Nieces
6 First cousins
7 Cripples
8 Second cousins
9 Invalids
10 Young-lady relations by marriage
11 Third cousins, and young-lady friends of the family
12 The Unclassified

Parties belonging to these twelve divisions should be saved in the order in which they are named.

The operator must keep himself utterly calm, and his line of procedure constantly in mind; otherwise the confusion around him will be almost sure to betray him into very embarrassing breaches of etiquette. Where there is much smoke, it is often quite difficult to distinguish between new Relatives by Marriage and Unclassified young ladies; wherefore it is provided that if the operator, in cases of this sort, shall rescue a No. 12 when he should have rescued a No. 10, it is not requisite that he carry No. 12 back again, but that he leave her where she is without remark, and go and fetch out No. 10. An apology to No. 10 is not imperative; still, it is good form to offer it. It may be deferred, however, one day— but no longer. [In a case of this nature which occurred during the first day of the Chicago fire, where the operator saved a No. 7 when a No. 6 was present but overlooked in the smoke, it was held by competent authorities, that the postponement of the apology for the extraordinary term of three days was justified, it being considered that the one-day term during which the apology must be offered means the day after the fire, and therefore does not begin *until the fire is out*. This decision was sustained by the several Illinois courts through which it was carried;

and experts are confident that it will also be sustained, eventually, in the Supreme Court of the United States—where it still lingers.]

To return to the fire.

Observe: 1's, 3's, 4's, and 5's may be *carried* out of the burning house, in the operator's arms—permission being first asked, and granted; 7's and 9's may be carried out without the formality of asking permission; the other grades may *not* be carried out, except they themselves take the initiative, and signify, by word or manner, their desire to partake of this attention.

Form for Requesting Permission to Carry a No. 1, 3, 4, or 5, out of a Boarding House Which Is on Fire.

The bonds of [here insert "tenderness," in the case of No. 1; or "blood," in the other cases] which enfold us in their silken tie, warrant me, my dear [here insert given name, in all cases; and without prefix], in offering to you the refuge of my arms in fleeing the fiery doom which now, with crimson wing, o'ershadows us.

In cases where a member of one of the prohibited grades signifies a desire to be carried out of the fire, response should be made in the following form—accompanied by a peculiarly profound obeisance:

Form of Response to Indication on the part of a 2, 6, 8, 10, 11 or 12 that she Desires to be Carried Out of a Fire in Arms of Young Gentleman.

In view of the circumstance, Madmoselle [insert *name* only in cases where the party is a 6 or an 8—be careful about this], that but fragile and conventional [here—in case of a No. 2—insert "Alas!"] are the bonds which enfold us in their silken tie, it is with deepest sense of the signal distinction which your condescension has conferred upon me, that I convey to you the refuge of my arms in fleeing the fiery doom which now, with crimson wing, o'ershadows us.

Other material in boarding house is to be rescued in the following order:

13 Babies
14 Children under 10 years of age
15 Young widows
16 Young married females
17 Elderly married ditto
18 Elderly widows
19 Clergymen
20 Boarders in general
21 Female domestics
22 Male ditto
23 Landlady
24 Landlord
25 Firemen
26 Furniture
27 Mothers-in-law

Arbitrary introductions, made under fire, to 12's through the necessity of carrying them out of the conflagration, are not binding. It rests with the young lady to renew the acquaintanceship or let it drop. If she shall desire the renewal, she may so signify by postal card; by intimation conveyed through friend of family; or by simple recognition of operator, by smile and slight inclination of head, the first time she meets him after the fire. In the resulting conversation the young gentleman must strictly refrain from introducing the subject of fire, or indeed of combustibles of any kind, lest he may seem to conceive and remember that he has lately done a heroic action, or at least an action meriting complimentary acknowledgment; whereas, on the contrary, he should studiedly seem to have forgotten the circumstance, until the young lady shall herself— if she so please—refer to it; in which case he will bow repeatedly, smiling continuously, and accompanying each bow with the observation (uttered in a soft, apparently embarrassed, yet gratified voice), "'m very glad, 'm sure, 'm very glad, 'm sure."

Offers of marriage to parties who are being carried out from a boarding house on fire are considered to be in questionable taste, for the reason that the subject of the proposition is not likely to be mistress of her best judgment at so alarming and confusing a time, and therefore it may chance that she is taken at a disadvantage. Indeed, the most authoritative canons of high breeding limit such offers inflexibly to cases where the respondent is a No. 2. In these instances, the following form should be observed:

Form of Offer of Marriage from Young Gentleman to a No. 2, during Process of Extracting Her from Boarding House on Fire, and Conveying Her out of the Same in His Arms.

Ah, I supplicate, I beseech, I implore thee, dearest [here insert given name of party only], to have compassion upon thy poor kneeling henchmen [do not attempt to kneel—this is but a figure of speech] and deign to be his! Deign to engender into bonds of tenderness those bonds of chill conventionality which enfold us in their silken tie, and he will ever bless the day thou didst accept the refuge of his arms in fleeing the fiery doom which now, with crimson wing, o'ershadows us.

Enough has been said, now, as to the conduct which a young gentleman of culture and breeding should observe in the case of a boarding house on fire. The same rules apply, with but slight variations (which will suggest themselves to the operator), to fire in a church, private house, hotel, railway train, or on shipboard—indeed to all fires in the ordinary walks of life.

In the case of a ship on fire, evening dress must be omitted. The true gentleman never wears evening dress at sea, even in case of a fire.

The speeches to be used at a fire may also, with but slight alteration, be wielded with effect upon disastrous occasions of other sorts. For instance, in tendering rescue from destruction by hurricane, or earthquake, or runaway team, or railway collision (where no conflagration ensues), the operator should merely substitute "fatal doom" for "fiery doom"; and in cases of ordinary shipwreck or other methods of drowning, he should say "watery doom." No other alterations are necessary, for the "crimson wing" applies to all calamities of a majestic sort, and is a phrase of exceeding finish and felicity.

Observe, in conclusion: Offers of marriage, during episode of run-away team, are to be avoided. A lady is sufficiently embarrassed at such a time; any act tending to add to this embarrassment is opposed to good taste, and therefore reprehensible.

THE LATE BENJAMIN FRANKLIN

Mark Twain

[*"**Never put off till tomorrow what
you can do day after tomorrow
just as well.**"—B. F.*]

This party was one of those persons whom they call Philosophers. He was
twins, being born simultaneously in two different houses in the city of
Boston. These houses remain unto this day, and have signs upon them
worded in accordance with the facts. The signs are considered well
enough to have, though not necessary, because the inhabitants point
out the two birthplaces to the stranger anyhow, and sometimes as often
as several times in the same day. The subject of this memoir was of a
vicious disposition, and early prostituted his talents to the invention of
maxims and aphorisms calculated to inflict suffering upon the rising
generation of all subsequent ages. His simplest acts, also, were contrived
with a view to their being held up for the emulation of boys forever—
boys who might otherwise have been happy. It was in this spirit that he
became the son of a soap-boiler, and probably for no other reason than
that the efforts of all future boys who tried to be anything might be
looked upon with suspicion unless they were the sons of soap-boilers.
With a malevolence which is without parallel in history, he would work
all day, and then sit up nights, and let on to be studying algebra by the
light of a smoldering fire, so that all other boys might have to do that
also, or else have Benjamin Franklin thrown up to them. Not satisfied
with these proceedings, he had a fashion of living wholly on bread and
water, and studying astronomy at mealtime—a thing which has brought
affliction to millions of boys since, whose fathers had read Franklin's
pernicious biography.

His maxims were full of animosity toward boys. Nowadays a boy cannot follow out a single natural instinct without tumbling over some of those everlasting aphorisms and hearing from Franklin on the spot. If he buys two cents' worth of peanuts, his father says, "Remember what Franklin has said, my son—'A groat a day's a penny a year'"; and the comfort is all gone out of those peanuts. If he wants to spin his top when he has done work, his father quotes, "Procrastination is the thief of time." If he does a virtuous action, he never gets anything for it, because "Virtue is its own reward." And that boy is hounded to death and robbed of his natural rest, because Franklin said once, in one of his inspired flights of malignity:

> Early to bed and early to rise
> Makes a man healthy and wealthy and wise.

As if it were any object to a boy to be healthy and wealthy and wise on such terms. The sorrow that that maxim has cost me, through my parents, experimenting on me with it, tongue cannot tell. The legitimate result is my present state of general debility, indigence, and mental aberration. My parents used to have me up before nine o'clock in the morning sometimes when I was a boy. If they had let me take my natural rest where would I have been now? Keeping store, no doubt, and respected by all.

And what an adroit old adventurer the subject of this memoir was! In order to get a chance to fly his kite on Sunday he used to hang a key on the string and let on to be fishing for lightning. And a guileless public would go home chirping about the "wisdom" and the "genius" of the hoary Sabbath-breaker. If anybody caught him playing "mumble-peg" by himself, after the age of sixty, he would immediately appear to be ciphering out how the grass grew—as if it was any of his business. My grandfather knew him well, and he says Franklin was always fixed—always ready. If a body, during his old age, happened on him unexpectedly when he was catching flies, or making mud pies, or sliding on a cellar door, he would immediately look wise, and rip out a maxim, and walk off with his nose in the air and his cap turned wrong side before, trying to appear absentminded and eccentric. He was a hard lot.

He invented a stove that would smoke your head off in four hours by the clock. One can see the almost devilish satisfaction he took in it by his giving it his name.

He was always proud of telling how he entered Philadelphia for the first time, with nothing in the world but two shillings in his pocket and four rolls of bread under his arm. But really, when you come to examine it critically, it was nothing. Anybody could have done it.

To the subject of this memoir belongs the honor of recommending the army to go back to bows and arrows in place of bayonets and muskets. He observed, with his customary force, that the bayonet was very well under some circumstances, but that he doubted whether it could be used with accuracy at a long range.

Benjamin Franklin did a great many notable things for his country, and made her young name to be honored in many lands as the mother of such a son. It is not the idea of this memoir to ignore that or cover it up. No; the simple idea of it is to snub those pretentious maxims of his, which he worked up with a great show of originality out of truisms that had become wearisome platitudes as early as the dispersion from Babel; and also to snub his stove, and his military inspirations, his unseemly endeavor to make himself conspicuous when he entered Philadelphia, and his flying his kite and fooling away his time in all sorts of such ways when he ought to have been foraging for soap-fat, or constructing candles. I merely desired to do away with somewhat of the prevalent calamitous idea among heads of families that Franklin *acquired* his great genius by working for nothing, studying by moonlight, and getting up in the night instead of waiting till morning like a Christian; and that this program, rigidly inflicted, will make a Franklin of every father's fool. It is time these gentlemen were finding out that these execrable eccentricities of instinct and conduct are only the *evidences* of genius, not the *creators* of it. I wish I had been the father of my parents long enough to make them comprehend this truth, and thus prepare them to let their son have an easier time of it. When I was a child I had to boil soap, notwithstanding my father was wealthy, and I had to get up early and study geometry at breakfast, and peddle my own poetry, and do everything just as Franklin did, in the solemn hope that I would be a Franklin some day. And here I am.

A FINE OLD MAN

Mark Twain

John Wagner, the oldest man in Buffalo—one hundred and four years old—recently walked a mile and a half in two weeks.

He is as cheerful and bright as any of these other old men that charge around so persistently and tiresomely in the newspapers, and in every way as remarkable.

Last November he walked five blocks in a rainstorm, without any shelter but an umbrella, and cast his vote for Grant, remarking that he had voted for forty-seven presidents—which was a lie.

His "second crop" of rich brown hair arrived from New York yesterday, and he has a new set of teeth coming—from Philadelphia.

He is to be married next week to a girl one hundred and two years old, who still takes in washing.

They have been engaged eighty years, but their parents persistently refused their consent until three days ago.

John Wagner is two years older than the Rhode Island veteran, and yet has never tasted a drop of liquor in his life—unless—unless you count whisky.

A PAGE FROM A CALIFORNIAN ALMANAC

Mark Twain

At the instance of several friends who feel a boding anxiety to know beforehand what sort of phenomena we may expect the elements to exhibit during the next month or two, and who have lost all confidence in the various patent medicine almanacs, because of the unaccountable reticence of those works concerning the extraordinary event of the 8th inst., I have compiled the following almanac expressly for the latitude of San Francisco:

OCT. 17 Weather hazy; atmosphere murky and dense. An expression of profound melancholy will be observable upon most countenances.

OCT. 18 Slight earthquake. Countenances grow more melancholy.

OCT. 19 Look out for rain. It would be absurd to look in for it. The general depression of spirits increased.

OCT. 20 More weather.

OCT. 21 Same.

OCT. 22 Light winds, perhaps. If they blow, it will be from the "east'ard, or the nor'ard, or the west'ard, or the suth'ard," or from some general direction approximating more or less to these points of the compass or otherwise. Winds are uncertain—more especially when they blow from whence they cometh and whither they listeth. N.B.—Such is the nature of winds.

OCT. 23 Mild, balmy earthquakes.

OCT. 24 Shaky.

OCT. 25 Occasional shakes, followed by light showers of bricks and plastering. N.B.—Stand from under!

OCT. 26 Considerable phenomenal atmospheric foolishness. About this time expect more earthquakes; but do not look for them, on account of the bricks.

OCT. 27 Universal despondency, indicative of approaching disaster. Abstain from smiling, or indulgence in humorous conversation, or exasperating jokes.

OCT. 28 Misery, dismal forebodings, and despair. Beware of all light discourse —a joke uttered at this time would produce a popular outbreak.

OCT. 29 Beware!

OCT. 30 Keep dark!

OCT. 31 Go slow!

NOV. 1 Terrific earthquake. This is the great earthquake month. More stars fall and more worlds are slathered around carelessly and destroyed in November than in any other month of the twelve.

NOV. 2 Spasmodic but exhilarating earthquakes, accompanied by occasional showers of rain and churches and things.

NOV. 3 Make your will.

NOV. 4 Sell out.

NOV. 5 Select your "last words." Those of John Quincy Adams will do, with the addition of a syllable, thus: "This is the last of earthquakes."

NOV. 6 Prepare to shed this mortal coil.

NOV. 7 Shed!

NOV. 8 The sun will rise as usual, perhaps; but if he does, he will doubtless be staggered some to find nothing but a large round hole eight thousand miles in diameter in the place where he saw this world serenely spinning the day before.

THE DISCOVERY
OF AMERICA

Richard Armour

America was founded by Columbus in 1492. This is an easy date to remember because it rhymes with "ocean blue," which was the color of the Atlantic in those days. If he had sailed a year later the date would still be easy to remember because it would rhyme with "boundless sea."

Columbus fled to this country because of persecution by Ferdinand and Isabella, who refused to believe the world was round, even when Columbus showed them an egg. Ferdinand later became famous because he objected to bullfights and said he preferred to smell flowers if he had to smell anything. He was stung in the end by a bee.

Before Columbus reached America, which he named after a man called American Vesuvius, he cried "Ceylon! Ceylon!" because he wanted to see India, which was engraved on his heart, before he died. When he arrived, he cried again. This time he cried "Excelsior!" meaning "I have founded it." Excelsior has been widely used ever since by persons returning with chinaware from China, with indiaware from India, and with underware from Down Under.

Columbus was mistaken in thinking he had reached India when actually he had not got even as far as Indiana. There is still a great deal of confusion about the East and the West. As Columbus discovered, if you go west long enough you find yourself in the east, and vice versa. The East and the West are kept apart by the Date Line, just as the North and South are kept apart by the Masons' Dixon Line. In the New World most of the eastern half of the country is called the Middle West, although it is known as the East by those who live in the Far West.

Columbus, who was as confused as anybody who has been at sea for a long time, called the first people he saw "Indians." It is not known what they called Columbus. His unfortunate error has been perpetuated

53

through the centuries. The original Americans are still known as "Indians," while all manner of immigrants from England, Ireland, Angora, and Liechtenstein are referred to as "Americans."[1]

Accompanied by his devoted followers, the Knights of Columbus, Columbus made several other voyages in search of India. Try as he might, however, he kept discovering America, and finally returned to Spain to die. He lived for a time in Madrid, but spent his last days in Disgrace.

A MINORITY OPINION

Some say it was not Columbus who discovered America but a man named Leaf Ericson. Leaf came from one of the Scandinavian countries with a shipload of people, all of whom were called Yon Yonson or Ole Olson or Big Swede, and went straight to Wisconsin, where he unloaded his passengers and went back for more.

On his next trip he went to Minnesota.

We know all this from some undecipherable remarks he made on a piece of stone. This stone has since become an utter rune.

FURTHER EXPLORATIONS

After Columbus proved the world was round, a great many people went around it. Marco Polo, who was one of the earlier explorers, had the misfortune to live several centuries before Columbus. Therefore, although he got around a good deal, he did not get completely around. He went far to the north, however, and is remembered for his discovery of the Polo regions.

The chief rivals in exploration were England and Spain. England had men like Cabot, who spoke only to a man named Lowell, and Sir Francis Drake, who had a singed beard and a ship called the *Golden Behind.*

Nor should we forget Sir Martin Fourflusher.[2]

[1]Or, by their mathematically inclined friends, "100 percent Americans."
[2]A direct descendant of the early Saxons, who knew all the Angles.

The struggle between England and Spain came to a climax in an epic sea battle off the Azores known as the Last Fight of the Revenge. In this decisive conflict, Sir Richard Grenville and Alfred Lord Tennyson proved conclusively that the lighter English warships could get more miles to the galleon.

England has ruled the waves ever since and has kept the sun from setting anywhere on her empire, thus providing a longer working day than in other countries.

STILL FURTHER EXPLORATIONS

Other explorers included Bilbo, Cabbage de Vaca, Cortez (known as The Stout, who traveled much in realms looking for gold), and Pantsy de Lion, a thirsty old man who was looking for a drinking fountain.[3] He never found it, but he founded Florida, to which a great many thirsty old men have gone ever since.

THE VIRGINIA COLONY

All this time there was not much happening in the New World, except that it was steadily growing older.

This period, known as the Doldrums, came to an end in fifteen-something-or-other when Sir Walter Raleigh, a man with a pointed beard and a pointless way of muddying his cloak, established a colony in America in the hope of pleasing the Queen, whose favor he had been in but was temporarily out of.

Although he claimed the new land in the name of Elizabeth, he called it Virginia, which aroused suspicions in Elizabeth's mind and caused her to confine Sir Walter in a tower. While imprisoned, Sir Walter made good use of his time by writing a history of the world on such scraps of paper as he could find, and filling other scraps of paper with a weed brought back from Virginia.

---

[3]Some historians say that in his wanderings through the South he invented the Dixie cup, just in case.

He had barely completed his history when he lost his head. Had he been permitted to keep it a few years longer he might have become the first man to roll a cigarette with one hand.

The Virginia Colony was lost for a time, and its name was changed to The Lost Colony, but it was subsequently found at about the place where it was last seen. Its original name of Virginia was restored because Elizabeth no longer cared, being dead.[4]

THE INDIANS

The people who were already in the New World when the white men arrived were the first Americans, or America Firsters. They were also referred to as the First Families of Virginia.

The early colonists found the Indians living in toupees, or wigwams, and sending up smoke signals, or wigwags, with piece pipes. Apparently because of a shortage of pipes, they sat in a circle and passed one pipe around, each biting off a piece as it passed. The chief Indian was named Hiawatha, and his squaw, whose name was Evangeline, did all the work. This was later to become an Old American Custom.

The Chiefs, it must be said in all fairness, were too busy to work. They were engaged in making wampum, or whoopee, when they were not mixing war paint or scattering arrowheads about, to be found centuries later.

In order to have their hands free to work, the squaws carried their babies, or cabooses, on their back, very much as kangaroos carry their babies on their front, only different.

The Indians were stern, silent people who never showed their feelings, even while being scalped. They crept up on their enemies without breaking a twig and were familiar with all the warpaths. Despite their savage ways, they sincerely loved peace, and were called Nobel Savages.

Their favorite word was "How," which the colonists soon learned was not a question.

The whites feared the redskins and considered them the forest's prime evil. Some went so far as to say that "The only good Indian is a wooden Indian." The redskins resented the whiteskins because they thought

---

[4]The end of Elizabeth is known as the Elizabethan Period.

they had come to take their lands away from them, and their fears were well grounded.

CAPTAIN JOHN SMITH

Captain John Smith was the first of a long line of Smiths who came to this country to keep up with the Joneses.

He was captured by the great Indian Chief, Powhatan, and was about to be killed when Popocatepetl, the fiery young daughter of the Chief, stepped in. We are not told what she stepped in, but she saved Captain John Smith's life, for which he thanked her. Later she married an Englishman, which improved relations.

THE PILGRIMS

The Pilgrims were a branch of the Puritans, and were proud of their family tree.[5] They wore tall hats, which they had to take off when they went inside because they attended a low church. This displeased King James, who raised the roof. He demanded that they attend the same church as he did. At least this is his side of the story, which became known as the King James Version.

Although the King insisted, the Puritans, who were very stiff-necked from years of wearing truffles on their collars, stubbornly declined. They would probably still be declining if they had not left England and gone to Leyden, a city in Holland noted for the discovery of electricity in a jar. (Electricity was subsequently lost for a while, but was rediscovered, by accident, when Benjamin Franklin was told to go fly a kite, and did.)

While in Holland, the Pilgrims suffered from pangs of sin,[6] and sent their children to Dutch Reform Schools when they misbehaved. These children, naturally enough, became Protestants, but their protests were ignored.

[5]These, it should be noted, were the first Puritans. The last Puritan was a Spanish nun named Santa Anna.

[6]Some years later a man named Sigmund Fraud claimed they enjoyed it.

THE PLYMOUTH COLONY

After several years in Holland, the Pilgrims decided to set out for the New World. This decision to move is known as Pilgrims' Progress.

The ship on which they sailed was the *Mayflower*. In stormy weather the women and children descended below the heaving decks, thus becoming the *Mayflower* descendants. There they huddled with the Colonial Dames and other early settlers and passed the weary hours comparing genealogies.

It was a long and perilous voyage across the Atlantic. Several times they were blown off their course. But finally, in 1620, which was a doubly Memorable Year because it was also the year in which they set sail, they sighted the rocky coast. The rock on which they landed they called Plymouth Rock because it reminded them of another rock of the same name in England. They built a small picket fence around it and made it a national shrine.

The first four men ashore became our fourfathers.

THE FIRST WINTER

After a short stay on Plymouth Rock, which was windy and damp, the Pilgrims sought a more sheltered place to build a town. One party went in one direction and one went in another. This was the beginning of the two-party system. When the two parties met, they held the first town meeting.

The first winter was cold,[7] which was a distinct surprise to the Pilgrims. Indeed, they might not have survived but for the corn that was given them by friendly Indians. By a curious quirk of history, it has since become illegal for white men to give Indians either corn or rye.

One thing that helped the Pilgrims get through the winter was the economical practice of putting young men and women into bed together, fully clothed. This odd practice, known as bungling, was endured by the young people of the colony until the weather became milder and a sufficient supply of bed-warmers could be imported from England.

[7]Probably responsible for the blue noses which became one of the Pilgrims' outstanding features.

The next spring the crops were good, and in the fall the Pilgrims cele-brated their first Thanksgiving, which fell, that fall, on a Thursday. The friendly Indians were invited, and the unfriendly Indians stayed in the background, muttering.

CAPTAIN MILES STANDISH

One of the leaders of the little band[8] at Plymouth was Captain Miles Standish. He was known throughout the township for his courtship.

He was an exceptional man. Except for him, almost all the Pilgrims were named William or John. One of the latter was Miles Standish's friend, quiet John Alden, a man who did not speak for himself until spoken to. He was spoken to, and sharply, by the fair Priscilla, whom he married, much to the annoyance of Miles Standish, who thought he was stood up by his stand-in.

THE COLONIES GROW

Let us leave the Pilgrims in Plymouth and see what was happening elsewhere in New England.

Education took a forward step with the founding of Harvard in a yard near the Charles River. Among the early benefactors of Harvard was a plantation owner from the South known as "Cotton" Mather. The first library was only a five-foot shelf, given to the college by T.S. Eliot, a graduate who no longer had need of it.[9] The books on this shelf are known as the Great Books and have grown to one hundred.

With the founding of two other old colleges, Old Eli and Old Nassau, the educational system was complete. Because of the ivory towers which were a distinctive feature of many of the early buildings, the three col-leges became known as the Ivory League.

To provide recreational facilities for students at Harvard, the city of

---

[8]A precursor of such bandleaders as Paul Whiteman and Benny Goodman.

[9]Having made a fortune in real estate by the sale of wasteland.

Boston was established. Boston became famous for its two famous hills, Beacon and Bunker, its two famous churches, North and South, and its two famous bays, Back and Front.

The people of Boston became wealthy by exporting baked beans and codfish, which they were smart enough not to eat themselves. Many, who were pillars of the church and pillars of society, came to be known as Proper Bostonians.

WILLIAMS AND PENN

One who was unhappy with life in Plymouth was Roger Williams, who thought the Pilgrims were intolerable. The Pilgrims, in turn, thought Williams was impossible. He proposed that they pay the Indians for their land instead of simply taking it from them. This utopian suggestion was dismissed by the Pilgrims as economically unsound.

Because of his unorthodox views, the Pilgrims branded him. They branded him a heretic, and drove him from town to town, although he preferred to walk. This was why Roger Williams reluctantly left Plymouth and founded Rhode Island, which is really not an island and is so small that it is usually indicated on maps by the letters "R.I." out in the Atlantic Ocean. It was once densely wooded. It is now densely populated.[10]

William Penn, on the other hand, came to America to collect some land the King owed his father. He belonged to a frightened religious sect known as the Quakers. So that he would not be forgotten, he gave his name to the Pennsylvania Railroad, the Pennsylvania Station, and the state prison, which is known as the Penn.

MASSACHUSETTS BAY

The English had always been a seafaring race, ever since they were Danes. Therefore one of their first acts in the New World was to make Massachusetts Bay a colony. From Massachusetts Bay and the nearby bayous they went out in their high-masted vessels looking for whale oil, which they found mostly in whales. The men who went away on voyages

[10]Many, with leftist political leanings, became Rhode Island Reds.

to capture whales were called whalers. So, by coincidence, were their sturdy ships. This is more confusing to us now than it was then.

The most famous whale, in those days, was an ill-tempered, unpredictable old whale called Moody Dick. Everyone was on the lookout for him, especially whalers whose legs he had bitten off in one of his nastier moods. The one-legged whaler who was most resentful was Captain A. Hab, who persisted until he finally managed to harpoon Moody Dick where it hurt the most. The whale had the last word, however, for he overturned Captain A. Hab's ship, the *Peapod,* which went down with all hands, including both of Captain A. Hab's.

CONNECTICUT

Fortunately for those who liked to visit New York but preferred not to live there, Connecticut was founded within commuting distance.

It was founded by Thomas Hooker, a clergyman who, in a dim church, interpreted the Gospel according to his own lights. He would also accept no money for his preaching, which set a low wage standard for others; he was therefore scorned as a free thinker. So he left under a cloud. Many of his parishioners believed his stern words about hell and followed him to Hartford, where he guaranteed them protection in the hereafter and sold them the first fire-insurance policies.

Connecticut is usually spelled Conn, which is easier.

LIFE IN OLD NEW ENGLAND

Most of the Puritans were ministers. Each week they could hardly wait until Sunday, when they preached for several hours on such subjects as "Hellfire" and "Damnation." In those days, church attendance was as good every Sunday as it is today on Easter.

All the Puritans, except a few who should never have left England, were opposed to sin. When a woman sinned, they pinned a scarlet letter "A" on her breast, where it would be conspicuous. Women who won their letter year after year were disdainfully called Scarlet, like Scarlet O'Hara and Scarlet Pimpernel. Children were kept in innocence of the meaning of the "A" and thought it stood for "Adulthood," when such things usually happened.

The homes of the Puritans were simple and austere, but their furniture was antique and therefore frightfully expensive. The chairs were as straight and stiff as the Puritans themselves, and had hard bottoms. They became known as period pieces because they went to pieces after a short period of sitting on them. The women had large chests or collector's items, of which they were extremely proud. Some of these have been handed down from generation to generation and are displayed proudly by their owners today.

Stores were known as Shoppes, or Ye Olde Shoppes. Prices were somewhat higher at the latter.

The Puritans believed in justice. A woman who was a witch, or a man who was a son of a witch, was punished by being stuck in the stocks. These were wooden devices that had holes to put the arms and legs through, and were considered disgraceful. They were also considered uncomfortable.

Every day the men went out into the fields in their blunderbusses and sowed corn. The women, meanwhile, were busy at home embroidering the alphabet and the date on a piece of cloth. One of the women, Hester Primmer, one of the New England Primmers, never got beyond the first letter of the alphabet. She also had only one date. That was with a young minister and was enough.

Other amusements were pillories, whipping posts, and Indian massacres.

THE LAND

The land was stony and hilly, except in places where it was hilly and stony. The stones were useful for making millstones and milestones. The Indians sharpened them and used them for scalping and other social purposes.

The hills were useful to watch for Indians from, unless the Indians were already on them. They were hard to plow up, but they were relatively easy to plow down.

THE CLIMATE

The winters in New England were long. Largely for this reason, the summers were short. In keeping with the seasons, long underwear was worn in the winter and short underwear in the summer.

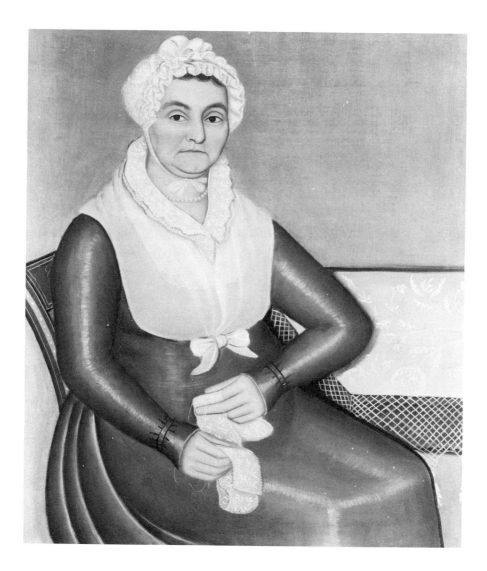

THE DUTCH AND THE FRENCH COME TO AMERICA

Many believed there was a shorter way to get to Asia than around America. Not yet having discovered the Panama Canal, they were looking for the next best thing, which was the Northwest Passage. Since it did not exist, it was, of course, hard to find. Nevertheless many Intrepid Explorers made their reputation hunting for it.

One of those who sought the Northwest Passage was Henry Hudson. In a ship of which he was part owner, called the *Half Mine,* he led a crew of Dutchmen to the mouth of the Hudson River, which he was pleased to find named after himself.

Stopping only to make friends with the Indians and to buy the island of Manhattan from an Indian named Minnehaha (or "Laughing Minnie") for a handful of beads,[11] he pushed on up the river. When he stopped pushing he was in Albany, and he was disappointed. The water was getting shallower and shallower and it was clear. It was clear that this was not the Northwest Passage, and that instead of founding an important route to the Orient, he was about to founder at the state capital. The choice was also clear. He must remain in Albany or make the hard and perilous voyage back across the Atlantic. Without hesitation he chose the latter.

On a second trip to the New World in search of the elusive Passage, Henry Hudson sailed into Hudson Bay. This, again, was not the Northwest Passage, but its name had a familiar ring.

It is not known what became of this Able Navigator who had not been able to find what he was looking for. One theory is that Hudson met Cadillac and De Soto, and that together they discovered Detroit.

NEW AMSTERDAM

Because of Henry Hudson's explorations, the Dutch laid claim to the mouth of the Hudson River, which in their systematic way they divided into the North River and the East River. A stubborn race, they named Manhattan New Amsterdam, although it was obviously New York.

[11]Beads were then selling at $24 a handful.

New Amsterdam was soon swarming with wealthy Dutch traitors known as poltroons. These were bluff, hearty men who smoked long pipes and loved to eat burghers. They frequently had their pictures painted, and one of the most picturesque was their Governor, Rip Van Wrinkle, a one-legged gentleman who fell into a deep sleep while watching a bowling game.

The English also claimed Manhattan, in view of the fact that the beads with which it was purchased were plainly stamped "Made in England." The Dutch could not see the merits of their claim, but they could see that the English had more guns on their warships, so they left.

This was a turning point.

The clever English changed the name Amsterdam to York, but they retained the New.[12]

LA SALLE

The French, although exhausted by the Hundred Years' War, were not too tired to try to establish themselves in the New World. There were still mountains which had not been planted with flags, and there were still rivers that had not been sailed up. So they sailed up them. Many of these still rivers ran deep and led into fastnesses where no white man had ever trod and very few had walked.

At last the only river remaining to be sailed up was the Mississippi. In this instance the French explorer La Salle defied convention. A headstrong young man, he began at the headwaters of the mighty river and sailed down it. He thus not only opened up a vast new territory but discovered an easier means of navigating the rivers of America. La Salle's interesting account of his trip down the river, called *Life on the Mississippi*, is available in an English translation by Mark Twain.

Thanks to La Salle, the Mississippi basin remained in French hands until they grew tired of holding it and sold it for $15,000,000, which many thought was a high price for a second-hand basin.

It is to the French also that we owe the establishment of the beautiful city of Quebec, which was named, according to custom, after the King of France, whose name, according to custom, was Louis (pronounced

[12]The city was later called New York, New York, for the sake of those who did not catch it the first time.

kwĕ-bĕk′). The English later seized Quebec and its outskirts, called Canada, from the French, but not without a struggle.

Henceforth the French were dominated by the English, who became our Good Neighbors to the north. We have had amicable relations ever since by agreeing that there are two sides to everything, for example Niagara Falls, which has an American side and a Canadian side.

FIRST TEST

1   Why do you think Columbus was so interested in traveling to distant places? What else do you know about his home life?

2   Are you really convinced that the world is round? Do you worry much about it?

3   To what extent would the course of American history have been altered if America had never been discovered?

4   What would you say about the Puritans? Would you say the same if they were listening?

5   Can the passengers on the *Mayflower* be considered immigrants? With their strong sense of duty, do you suppose they tried to conceal anything from the customs officials?

6   Have you ever thought how much of a Pilgrim was wasted when an Indian kept only his scalp?

7   Trace on a map the voyages of Henry Hudson. Use a solid line to show where he went and a dotted line to show where he thought he was going. Sign on the dotted line.

8   What would you have done if you had been in La Salle's shoes? How do you know he wore any?

The leopard with the harmless kid laid down,
And not one savage beast was seen to frown.

The lion with the fatling on did move,
A little child was leading them in love.

The wolf did with the lambkin dwell in peace.
His grim carnivrous nature there did cease.

When the great PENN his famous treaty made,
With indian chiefs beneath the elm-trees shade.

A Receipt To Make a New-England Funeral Elegy

Benjamin Franklin

From "Dogood Papers," No. VII, a series of humorous aricles written by Benjamin Franklin under the pen name, Silence Dogood. Published in *The New England Courant*, a Boston newspaper published by Franklin's brother, in 1722.

. . . For the Subject of your Elegy. Take one of your Neighbours who has lately departed this Life; it is no great matter at what Age the Party dy'd, but it will be best if he went away suddenly, being Kill'd, Drown'd, or Frose to Death.

Having chose the Person, take all his Virtues, Excellencies, etc. and if he have not enough, you may borrow some to make up a sufficient Quantity: To these add his last Words, dying Expressions, etc., if they are to be had; mix all these together, and be sure you strain them well. Then season all with a Handful or two of Melancholly Expressions, such as, Dreadful, Deadly, cruel cold Death, unhappy Fate, weeping Eyes, etc. . . . let them Ferment for the Space of a Fortnight, and by that Time they will be incorporated into a Body, which take out, and having prepared a sufficient Quantity of double Rhimes, such as Power, Flower; Quiver, Shiver; Grieve us, Leave us; tell you, excel you; Expeditions, Physicians; Fatigue him, Intrigue him; etc., you must spread all upon Paper, and if you can procure a Scrap of Latin to put at the End, it will garnish it mightily; then having affixed your Name at the Bottom, . . . you will have an Excellent Elegy.

N.B. This Receipt will serve when a Female is the Subject of your Elegy, provided you borrow a greater Quantity of Virtues, Excellencies, etc.

Sir,

Your Servant,
SILENCE DOGOOD.

THE RANSOM
OF RED CHIEF

O. Henry

It looked like a good thing; but wait till I tell you. We were down South, in Alabama—Bill Driscoll and myself—when this kidnapping idea struck us. It was, as Bill afterward expressed it, "during a moment of temporary mental apparition"; but we didn't find that out till later.

There was a town down there, as flat as flannel-cake, and called Summit, of course. It contained inhabitants of as undeleterious and self-satisfied a class of peasantry as ever clustered around a Maypole.

Bill and me had a joint capital of about $600, and we needed just $2000 more to pull off a fraudulent town-lot scheme in Western Illinois with. We talked it over on the front steps of the hotel. Philoprogenitiveness, says we, is strong in semirural communities; therefore, and for other reasons, a kidnapping project ought to do better there than in the radius of newspapers that send reporters out in plain clothes to stir up talk about such things. We knew that Summit couldn't get after us with anything stronger than constables, and, maybe, some lackadaisical bloodhounds and a diatribe or two in the *Weekly Farmers' Budget.* So it looked good.

We selected for our victim the only child of a prominent citizen named Ebenezer Dorset. The father was respectable and tight, a mortgage fancier and a stern, upright collection-plate passer and forecloser. The kid was a boy of ten, with bas-relief freckles, and hair the color of the cover of the magazine you buy at the newsstand when you want to catch a train. Bill and me figured that Ebenezer would melt down for a ransom of $2000 to a cent. But wait till I tell you.

About two miles from Summit was a little mountain, covered with a dense cedar brake. On the rear elevation of this mountain was a cave. There we stored provisions.

One evening after sundown we drove in a buggy past old Dorset's house. The kid was in the street, throwing rocks at a kitten on the opposite fence.

"Hey, little boy!" says Bill, "would you like to have a bag of candy and a nice ride?"

The boy catches Bill neatly in the eye with a piece of brick.

"That will cost the old man an extra five hundred dollars," says Bill, climbing over the wheel.

That boy put up a fight like a welterweight cinnamon bear; but at last we got him down in the bottom of the buggy and drove away. We took him up to the cave, and I hitched the horse in the cedar brake. After dark I drove the buggy to the little village, three miles away, where we had hired it, and walked back to the mountain.

Bill was pasting court plaster over the scratches and bruises on his features. There was a fire burning behind the big rock at the entrance of the cave, and the boy was watching a pot of boiling coffee, with two buzzard-tail feathers stuck in his red hair. He points a stick at me when I come up, and says:

"Ha! Cursed paleface, do you dare to enter the camp of Red Chief, the terror of the plains?"

"He's all right now," says Bill, rolling up his trousers and examining some bruises on his shins. "We're playing Indian. We're making Buffalo Bill's show look like magic-lantern views of Palestine in the town hall. I'm Old Hank, the Trapper, Red Chief's captive, and I'm to be scalped at daybreak. By Geronimo! That kid can kick hard."

Yes, sir, that boy seemed to be having the time of his life. The fun of camping out in a cave had made him forget that he was a captive himself. He immediately christened me Snake-eye the Spy, and announced that, when his braves returned from the warpath, I was to be broiled at the stake at the rising of the sun.

Then we had supper, and he filled his mouth full of bacon and bread and gravy, and began to talk. He made a during-dinner speech something like this:

"I like this fine. I never camped out before; but I had a pet 'possum once, and I was nine last birthday. I hate to go to school. Rats ate up sixteen of Jimmy Talbot's aunt's speckled hen's eggs. Are there any real Indians in these woods? I want some more gravy. Does the trees moving make the wind blow? We had five puppies. What makes your nose so red, Hank? My father has lots of money. Are the stars hot? I whipped Ed Walker twice, Saturday. I don't like girls. You dassent catch toads unless with a string. Do oxen make any noise? Why are oranges round? Have you got beds to sleep on in this cave? Amos Murray has got six toes. A parrot can talk, but a monkey or a fish can't. How many does it take to make twelve?"

Every few minutes he would remember that he was a pesky redskin, and pick up his stick rifle and tiptoe to the mouth of the cave to rubber for the scouts of the hated paleface. Now and then he would let out a war whoop that made Old Hank the Trapper shiver. The boy had Bill terrorized from the start.

"Red Chief," says I to the kid, "would you like to go home?"

"Aw, what for?" says he. "I don't have any fun at home. I hate to go to school. I like to camp out. You won't take me back home again, Snake-eye, will you?"

"Not right away," says I. "We'll stay here in the cave a while."

"All right!" says he. "That'll be fine. I never had such fun in all my life."

We went to bed about 11 o'clock. We spread down some wide blankets and quilts and put Red Chief between us. We weren't afraid he'd run away. He kept us awake for three hours, humping up and reaching for his rifle and screeching: "Hist! pard," in mine and Bill's ears, as the fancied crackle of a twig or the rustle of a leaf revealed to his young imagination the stealthy approach of the outlaw band. At last, I fell into a troubled sleep, and dreamed that I had been kidnapped and chained to a tree by a ferocious pirate with red hair.

Just at daybreak I was awakened by a series of awful screams from Bill. They weren't yells, or howls, or shouts, or whoops, or yawps, such as you'd expect from a manly set of vocal organs—they were simply indecent, terrifying, humiliating screams, such as women emit when they see ghosts or caterpillars. It's an awful thing to hear a strong, desperate, fat man scream incontinently in a cave at daybreak.

I jumped up to see what the matter was. Red Chief was sitting on Bill's chest, with one hand twined in Bill's hair. In the other he had the sharp case knife we used for slicing bacon; and he was industriously and realistically trying to take Bill's scalp, according to the sentence that had been pronounced upon him the evening before.

I got the knife away from the kid and made him lie down again. But from that moment Bill's spirit was broken. He laid down on his side of the bed, but he never closed an eye again in sleep as long as that boy was with us. I dozed for a while, but along toward sunup I remembered that Red Chief had said I was to be burned at the stake at the rising of the sun. I wasn't nervous or afraid, but I sat up and lit my pipe and leaned against a rock.

"What you getting up so soon for, Sam?" asked Bill.

"Me?" says I. "Oh, I got a kind of a pain in my shoulder. I thought sitting up would rest it."

"You're a liar!" says Bill. "You're afraid. You was to be burned at sunrise, and you was afraid he'd do it. And he would, too, if he could find a match. Ain't it awful, Sam? Do you think anybody will pay out money to get a little imp like that back home?"

"Sure," said I. "A rowdy kid like that is just the kind that parents dote on. Now, you and the Chief get up and cook breakfast, while I go up on the top of this mountain and reconnoiter."

I went up on the peak of the little mountain and ran my eye over the contiguous vicinity. Over toward Summit I expected to see the sturdy yeomanry of the village armed with scythes and pitchforks beating the countryside for the dastardly kidnappers. But what I saw was a peaceful landscape dotted with one man ploughing with a dun mule. Nobody was dragging the creek; no couriers dashed hither and yon, bringing tidings of no news to the distracted parents. There was a sylvan attitude of somnolent sleepiness pervading that section of the external outward surface of Alabama that lay exposed to my view. "Perhaps," says I to myself, "it has not yet been discovered that the wolves have borne away the tender lambkin from the fold. Heaven help the wolves!" says I, and went down the mountain to breakfast.

When I got to the cave I found Bill backed up against the side of it, breathing hard, and the boy threatening to smash him with a rock half as big as a coconut.

"He put a red-hot boiled potato down my back," explained Bill, "and then mashed it with his foot; and I boxed his ears. Have you got a gun about you, Sam?"

I took the rock away from the boy and kind of patched up the argument. "I'll fix you," says the kid to Bill. "No man ever yet struck the

Red Chief but what he got paid for it. You better beware!"

After breakfast the kid takes a piece of leather with strings wrapped around it out of his pocket and goes outside the cave unwinding it.

"What's he up to now?" says Bill anxiously. "You don't think he'll run away, do you, Sam?"

"No fear of it," says I. "He don't seem to be much of a homebody. But we've got to fix up some plan about the ransom. There don't seem to be much excitement around Summit on account of his disappearance; but maybe they think he's spending the night with Aunt Jane or one of the neighbors. Anyhow, he'll be missed today. Tonight we must get a message to his father demanding the two thousand dollars for his return."

Just then we heard a kind of war whoop, such as David might have emitted when he knocked out the champion Goliath. It was a sling that Red Chief had pulled out of his pocket, and he was whirling it around his head.

I dodged, and heard a heavy thud and a kind of a sigh from Bill, like a horse gives out when you take his saddle off. A rock the size of an egg had caught Bill just behind his left ear. He loosened himself all over and fell in the fire across the frying pan of hot water for washing the dishes. I dragged him out and poured cold water on his head for half an hour.

By and by, Bill sits up and feels behind his ear and says: "Sam, do you know who my favorite Biblical character is?"

"Take it easy," says I. "You'll come to your senses presently."

"King Herod," says he. "You won't go away and leave me here alone, will you, Sam?"

I went out and caught that boy and shook him until his freckles rattled.

"If you don't behave," says, I, "I'll take you straight home. Now, are you going to be good, or not?"

"I was only funning," says he sullenly. "I didn't mean to hurt Old Hank. But what did he hit me for? I'll behave, Snake-eye, if you won't send me home, and if you'll let me play the Black Scout today."

"I don't know the game," says I. "That's for you and Mr. Bill to decide. He's your playmate for the day. I'm going away for a while, on business. Now, you come in and make friends with him and say you are sorry for hurting him, or home you go, at once."

I made him and Bill shake hands, and then I took Bill aside and told him I was going to Poplar Cove, a little village three miles from the cave, and find out what I could about how the kidnapping had been regarded in Summit. Also, I thought it best to send a peremptory letter to old man Dorset that day, demanding the ransom and dictating how it should be paid.

"You know, Sam," says Bill, "I've stood by you without batting an eye in earthquakes, fire, and flood—in poker games, dynamite outrages, police raids, train robberies, and cyclones. I never lost my nerve yet till we kidnapped that two-legged skyrocket of a kid. He's got me going. You won't leave me long with him, will you, Sam?"

"I'll be back sometime this afternoon," says I. "You must keep the boy amused and quiet till I return. And now we'll write the letter to old Dorsey."

Bill and I got paper and pencil and worked on the letter while Red Chief, with a blanket wrapped around him, strutted up and down, guarding the mouth of the cave. Bill begged me tearfully to make the ransom $1500 instead of $2000. "I ain't attempting," says he, "to decry the celebrated moral aspect of parental affection, but we're dealing with humans, and it ain't human for anybody to give up two thousand dollars for that forty-pound chunk of freckled wildcat. I'm willing to take a chance at fifteen hundred dollars. You can charge the difference up to me."

So, to relieve Bill, I acceded, and we collaborated a letter that ran this way:

Ebenezer Dorset, Esq.:

We have your boy concealed in a place far from Summit. It is useless for you or the most skilled detectives to attempt to find him. Absolutely the only terms on which you can have him restored to you are these: We demand $1500 in large bills for his return: the money to be left at midnight at the same spot and in the same box as your reply—as hereinafter described. If you agree to these terms, send your answer in writing by a solitary messenger tonight at half-past eight o'clock. After crossing Owl Creek, on the road to Poplar Cove, there are three large trees about a hundred yards apart, close to the fence of the wheat field on the right-hand side. At the bottom of the fence post opposite the third tree will be found a small pasteboard box.

The messenger will place the answer in this box and return immediately to Summit.

If you attempt any treachery or fail to comply with our demand as stated, you will never see your boy again.

If you pay the money as demanded, he will be returned to you safe and well within three hours. These terms are final, and if you do not accede to them no further communication will be attempted.

Two Desperate Men

I addressed this letter to Dorset, and put it in my pocket. As I was about to start, the kid comes up to me and says:

"Aw, Snake-eye, you said I could play the Black Scout while you was gone."

"Play it, of course," says I. "Mr. Bill will play with you. What kind of a game is it?"

"I'm the Black Scout," says the Red Chief, "and I have to ride to the stockade to warn the settlers that the Indians are coming. I'm tired of playing Indian myself. I want to be the Black Scout."

"All right," says I. "It sounds harmless to me. I guess Mr. Bill will help you foil the pesky savages."

"What am I to do?" asks Bill, looking at the kid suspiciously.

"You are the hoss," says Black Scout. "Get down on your hands and knees. How can I ride to the stockade without a hoss?"

"You'd better keep him interested," said I, "till we get the scheme going. Loosen up."

Bill gets down on his all fours, and a look comes in his eye like a rabbit's when you catch it in a trap.

"How far is it to the stockade, kid?" he asks, in a husky manner of voice.

"Ninety miles," says the Black Scout. "And you have to hump yourself to get there on time. Whoa, now!"

The Black Scout jumps on Bill's back and digs his heels in his side.

"For heaven's sake," says Bill, "hurry back, Sam, as soon as you can. I wish we hadn't made the ransom more than a thousand. Say, you quit kicking me or I'll get up and warm you good."

I walked over to Poplar Cove and sat around the post office and store, talking with the chawbacons that came in to trade. One whiskerando says that he hears Summit is all upset on account of Elder Ebenezer Dorset's boy having been lost or stolen. That was all I wanted to know. I bought some smoking tobacco, referred casually to the price of black-eyed peas, posted my letter surreptitiously and came away. The post-master said the mail carrier would come by in an hour to take the mail on to Summit.

When I got back to the cave Bill and the boy were not to be found. I explored the vicinity of the cave, and risked a yodel or two, but there was no response.

So I lighted my pipe and sat down on a mossy bank to await developments.

In about half an hour I heard the bushes rustle, and Bill wobbled out into the little glade in front of the cave. Behind him was the kid, stepping softly like a scout, with a broad grin on his face. Bill stopped, took off his hat and wiped his face with a red handkerchief. The kid stopped about eight feet behind him.

"Sam," says Bill, "I suppose you think I'm a renegade, but I couldn't help it. I'm a grown person with masculine proclivities and habits of self-defense, but there is a time when all systems of egotism and pre-dominance fail. The boy is gone. I have sent him home. All is off. There was martyrs in old times," goes on Bill, "that suffered death rather than give up the particular graft they enjoyed. None of 'em was subjugated to such supernatural tortures as I have been. I tried to be faithful to our articles of depredation; but there came a limit."

"What's the trouble, Bill?" I asks him.

"I was rode," says Bill, "the ninety miles to the stockade, not barring an inch. Then, when the settlers was rescued, I was given oats. Sand ain't a palatable substitute. And then, for an hour I had to try to explain to him why there was nothin' in holes, how a road can run both ways and what makes the grass green. I tell you, Sam, a human can only stand so much. I takes him by the neck of his clothes and drags him down the mountain. On the way he kicks my legs black-and-blue from the knees down; and I've got to have two or three bites on my thumb and hand cauterized.

"But he's gone—" continues Bill—"gone home. I showed him the road to Summit and kicked him about eight feet nearer there at one kick. I'm sorry we lose the ransom; but it was either that or Bill Driscoll to the madhouse."

Bill is puffing and blowing, but there is a look of ineffable peace and growing content on his rose-pink features.

"Bill," says I, "there isn't any heart disease in your family, is there?"

"No," says Bill, "nothing chronic except malaria and accidents. Why?"

"Then you might turn around," says I, "and have a look behind you."

Bill turns and sees the boy, and loses his complexion and sits down plump on the ground and begins to pluck aimlessly at grass and little sticks. For an hour I was afraid of his mind. And then I told him that my scheme was to put the whole job through immediately and that we would get the ransom and be off with it by midnight if old Dorset fell in with our proposition. So Bill braced up enough to give the kid a weak sort of smile and a promise to play the Russian in a Japanese war with him as soon as he felt a little better.

I had a scheme for collecting that ransom without danger of being caught by counterplots that ought to commend itself to professional kidnappers. The tree under which the answer was to be left—and the money later on—was close to the road fence with big, bare fields on all sides. If a gang of constables should be watching for anyone to come for the note they could see him a long way off crossing the fields or in the road. But no, siree! At half past eight I was up in that tree as well hidden as a tree toad, waiting for the messenger to arrive.

Exactly on time, a half-grown boy rides up the road on a bicycle, locates the pasteboard box at the foot of the fence post, slips a folded piece of paper into it and pedals away again back toward Summit.

I waited an hour and then concluded the thing was square. I slid down the tree, got the note, slipped along the fence till I struck the woods, and was back at the cave in another half an hour. I opened the note, got near the lantern and read it to Bill. It was written with a pen in a crabbed hand, and the sum and substance of it was this:

Two Desperate Men

Gentlemen: I received your letter today by post, in regard to the ransom you ask for the return of my son. I think you are a little high in your demands, and I hereby make you a counterproposition, which I am inclined to believe you will accept. You bring Johnny home and pay me $250 in cash, and I agree to take him off your hands. You had better come at night, for the neighbors believe he is lost, and I couldn't be responsible for what they would do to anybody they saw bringing him back.

Very respectfully,

Ebenezer Dorset

"Great pirates of Penzance!" says I. "Of all the impudent—"

But I glanced at Bill, and hesitated. He had the most appealing look in his eyes I ever saw on the face of a dumb or talking brute.

"Sam," says he, "what's two hundred and fifty dollars, after all? We've got the money. One more night of this kid will send me to bed in Bedlam. Besides being a thorough gentleman, I think Mr. Dorset is a spendthrift for making us such a liberal offer. You ain't going to let the chance go, are you?"

"Tell you the truth, Bill," says I, "this little he ewe lamb has somewhat got on my nerves, too. We'll take him home, pay the ransom, and make our getaway."

We took him home that night. We got him to go by telling him that his father had bought a silver-mounted rifle and a pair of moccasins for him, and we were going to hunt bears the next day.

It was just 12 o'clock when we knocked at Ebenezer's front door. Just at the moment when I should have been abstracting the $1500 from the box under the tree, according to the original proposition, Bill was counting out $250 into Dorset's hand.

When the kid found out we were going to leave him at home he started up a howl like a calliope and fastened himself as tight as a leech to Bill's leg. His father peeled him away gradually, like a porous plaster.

"How long can you hold him?" asks Bill.

"I'm not as strong as I used to be," says old Dorset, "but I think I can promise you ten minutes."

"Enough," says Bill. "In ten minutes I shall cross the central, southern, and middle western states, and be legging it trippingly for the Canadian border."

And, as dark as it was, and as fat as Bill was, and as good a runner as I am, he was a good mile and a half out of Summit before I could catch up with him.

THE SECRET LIFE OF WALTER MITTY

James Thurber

"We're going through!" The Commander's voice was like thin ice breaking. He wore his full-dress uniform, with the heavily braided white cap pulled down rakishly over one cold gray eye. "We can't make it, sir. It's spoiling for a hurricane, if you ask me." "I'm not asking you, Lieutenant Berg," said the Commander. "Throw on the power lights! Rev her up to 8,500! We're going through!" The pounding of the cylinders increased: ta-pocketa-pocketa-pocketa-*pocketa-pocketa*. The Commander stared at the ice forming on the pilot window. He walked over and twisted a row of complicated dials. "Switch on No. 8 auxiliary!" he shouted. "Switch on No. 8 auxiliary!" repeated Lieutenant Berg. "Full strength in No. 3 turret!" shouted the Commander. "Full strength in No. 3 turret!" The crew, bending to their various tasks in the huge, hurtling eight-engined Navy hydroplane, looked at each other and grinned. "The Old Man'll get us through," they said to one another. "The Old Man ain't afraid of Hell!" . . .

"Not so fast! You're driving too fast!" said Mrs. Mitty. "What are you driving so fast for?"

"Hmm?" said Walter Mitty. He looked at his wife, in the seat beside him, with shocked astonishment. She seemed grossly unfamiliar, like a strange woman who had yelled at him in a crowd. "You were up to fifty-five," she said. "You know I don't like to go more than forty. You were up to fifty-five." Walter Mitty drove on toward Waterbury in silence, the roaring of the SN202 through the worst storm in twenty years of Navy flying fading in the remote, intimate airways of his mind. "You're tensed up again," said Mrs. Mitty. "It's one of your days. I wish you'd let Dr. Renshaw look you over."

Walter Mitty stopped the car in front of the building where his wife went to have her hair done. "Remember to get those overshoes while I'm having my hair done," she said. "I don't need overshoes," said

Mitty. She put her mirror back into her bag. "We've been all through that," she said, getting out of the car. "You're not a young man any longer." He raced the engine a little. "Why don't you wear your gloves? Have you lost your gloves?" Walter Mitty reached in a pocket and brought out the gloves. He put them on, but after she had turned and gone into the building and he had driven on to a red light, he took them off again. "Pick it up, brother!" snapped a cop as the light changed, and Mitty hastily pulled on his gloves and lurched ahead. He drove around the streets aimlessly for a time, and then he drove past the hospital on his way to the parking lot.

. . . "It's the millionaire banker, Wellington McMillan," said the pretty nurse. "Yes," said Walter Mitty, removing his gloves slowly. "Who has the case?" "Dr. Renshaw and Dr. Benbow, but there are two specialists here, Dr. Remington from New York and Mr. Pritchard-Mitford from London. He flew over." A door opened down a long, cool corridor and Dr. Renshaw came out. He looked distraught and haggard. "Hello, Mitty," he said. "We're having the devil's own time with McMillan, the millionaire banker and close personal friend of Roosevelt. Obstreosis of the ductal tract. Tertiary. Wish you'd take a look at him." "Glad to," said Mitty.

In the operating room there were whispered introductions: "Dr. Remington, Dr. Mitty. Mr. Pritchard-Mitford, Dr. Mitty." "I've read your book on streptothricosis," said Pritchard-Mitford, shaking hands. "A brilliant performance, sir." "Thank you," said Walter Mitty. "Didn't know you were in the States, Mitty," grumbled Remington. "Coals to Newcastle, bringing Mitford and me up here for a tertiary." "You are very kind," said Mitty. A huge, complicated machine, connected to the operating table, with many tubes and wires, began at this moment to go pocketa-pocketa-pocketa. "The new anesthetizer is giving way!" shouted an interne. "There is no one in the East who knows how to fix it!" "Quiet, man!" said Mitty, in a low, cool voice. He sprang to the machine, which was now going pocketa-pocketa-queep-pocketa-queep. He began fingering delicately a row of glistening dials. "Give me a fountain pen!" he snapped. Someone handed him a fountain pen. He pulled a faulty piston out of the machine and inserted the pen in its place. "That will hold for ten minutes," he said. "Get on with the operation." A nurse hurried over and whispered to Renshaw, and Mitty saw the man turn pale. "Coreopsis has set in," said Renshaw nervously. "If you would take over, Mitty?" Mitty looked at him and at the craven figure of Benbow, who drank, and at the grave, uncertain faces of the two great specialists. "If you wish," he said. They slipped a white gown on him; he adjusted a mask and drew on thin gloves; nurses handed him shining . . .

"Back it up, Mac! Look out for that Buick!" Walter Mitty jammed on the brakes. "Wrong lane, Mac," said the parking-lot attendant, looking at Mitty closely. "Gee. Yea," muttered Mitty. He began cautiously to back out of the lane marked "Exit Only." "Leave her sit there," said the attendant. "I'll put her away." Mitty got out of the car. "Hey, better leave the key." "Oh," said Mitty, handing the man the ignition key. The attendant vaulted into the car, backed it up with insolent skill, and put it where it belonged.

They're so damn cocky, thought Walter Mitty, walking along Main Street; they think they know everything. Once he had tried to take his chains off, outside New Milford, and he had got them wound around the axles. A man had had to come out in a wrecking car and unwind them, a young, grinning garageman. Since then Mrs. Mitty always made him drive to a garage to have the chains taken off. The next time, he thought, I'll wear my right arm in a sling; they won't grin at me then. I'll have my right arm in a sling and they'll see I couldn't possibly take the chains off myself. He kicked at the slush on the sidewalk. "Overshoes," he said to himself, and he began looking for a shoe store.

When he came out into the street again, with the overshoes in a box under his arm, Walter Mitty began to wonder what the other thing was his wife had told him to get. She had told him twice, before they set out from their house for Waterbury. In a way he hated these weekly trips to town—he was always getting something wrong. Kleenex, he thought, Squibb's, razor blades? No. Toothpaste, toothbrush, bicarbonate, carborundum, initiative and referendum? He gave it up. But she would remember it. "Where's the what's-its-name?" she would ask. "Don't tell me you forgot the what's-its-name." A newsboy went by shouting something about the Waterbury trial.

. . . "Perhaps this will refresh your memory." The District Attorney suddenly thrust a heavy automatic at the quiet figure on the witness stand. "Have you ever seen this before?" Walter Mitty took the gun and examined it expertly. "This is my Webley-Vickers 50.80," he said calmly. An excited buzz ran around the courtroom. The judge rapped for order.

"You are a crack shot with any sort of firearms, I believe?" said the District Attorney, insinuatingly. "Objection!" shouted Mitty's attorney. "We have shown that the defendant could not have fired the shot. We have shown that he wore his right arm in a sling on the night of the fourteenth of July." Walter Mitty raised his hand briefly and the bickering attorneys were stilled. "With any known make of gun," he said evenly, "I could have killed Gregory Fitzhurst at three hundred feet *with my left hand.*" Pandemonium broke loose in the courtroom. A woman's scream rose above the bedlam and suddenly a lovely, dark-haired girl was in Walter Mitty's arms. The District Attorney struck at her savagely. Without rising from his chair, Mitty let the man have it on the point of the chin. "You miserable cur!". . .

"Puppy biscuit," said Walter Mitty. He stopped walking and the buildings of Waterbury rose up out of the misty courtroom and surrounded him again. A woman who was passing laughed. "He said 'Puppy biscuit,'" she said to her companion. "That man said 'Puppy biscuit' to himself." Walter Mitty hurried on. He went into an A. & P., not the first one he came to but a smaller one farther up the street. "I want some biscuit for small, young dogs," he said to the clerk. "Any special brand, sir?" The greatest pistol shot in the world thought a moment. "It says 'Puppies Bark for It' on the box," said Walter Mitty.

His wife would be through at the hairdresser's in fifteen minutes, Mitty saw in looking at his watch, unless they had trouble drying it; sometimes they had trouble drying it. She didn't like to get to the hotel first; she would want him to be there waiting for her as usual. He found a big leather chair in the lobby, facing a window, and he put the overshoes and the puppy biscuit on the floor beside it. He picked up an old copy of *Liberty* and sank down into the chair. "Can Germany Conquer the World Through the Air?" Walter Mitty looked at the pictures of bombing planes and of ruined streets.

. . . "The cannonading has got the wind up in young Raleigh, sir," said the sergeant. Captain Mitty looked up at him through tousled hair. "Get him to bed," he said wearily. "With the others. I'll fly alone." "But you can't, sir," said the sergeant anxiously. "It takes two men to handle that bomber and the Archies are pounding hell out of the air. Von Richtman's circus is between here and Saulier." "Somebody's got to get that ammunition dump," said Mitty. "I'm going over. Spot of brandy?" He poured a drink for the sergeant and one for himself. War thundered and whined around the dugout and battered at the door. There was a rending of wood and splinters flew through the room. "A bit of a near thing," said Captain Mitty carelessly. "The box barrage is closing in," said the sergeant. "We only live once, Sergeant," said Mitty, with his faint, fleeting smile. "Or do we?" He poured another brandy and tossed it off. "I never see a man could hold his brandy like you, sir," said the sergeant. Begging your pardon, sir." Captain Mitty stood up and strapped on his huge Webley-Vickers automatic. "It's forty kilometers through hell, sir," said the sergeant. Mitty finished one last brandy. "After all," he said softly, "what isn't?" The pounding of the cannon increased; there was the rat-tat-tatting of machine guns, and from some-where came the menacing pocketa-pocketa-pocketa of the new flame-throwers. Walter Mitty walked to the door of the dugout humming "Auprès de Ma Blonde." He turned and waved to the sergeant. "Cheer-io!" he said. . . .

Something struck his shoulder. "I've been looking all over this hotel for you," said Mrs. Mitty. "Why do you have to hide in this old chair? How did you expect me to find you?" "Things close in," said Walter Mitty vaguely. "What?" Mrs. Mitty said. "Did you get the what's-its-name? The puppy biscuit? What's in that box?" "Overshoes," said Mitty. "Couldn't you have put them on in the store?" "I was thinking," said Walter Mitty. "Does it ever occur to you that I am sometimes think-ing?" She looked at him. "I'm going to take your temperature when I get you home," she said.

They went out through the revolving doors that made a faintly deri-sive whistling sound when you pushed them. It was two blocks to the parking lot. At the drugstore on the corner she said, "Wait here for me. I forgot something. I won't be a minute." She was more than a minute. Walter Mitty lighted a cigarette. It began to rain, rain with sleet in it. He stood up against the wall of the drugstore, smoking. . . . He put his shoulders back and his heels together. "To hell with the handker-chief," said Walter Mitty scornfully. He took one last drag on his ciga-rette and snapped it away. Then, with that faint, fleeting smile playing about his lips, he faced the firing squad; erect and motionless, proud and disdainful, Walter Mitty the Undefeated, inscrutable to the last.

FABLE IX

William Saroyan

*The Tribulations of the Simple Husband Who Wanted Nothing More than to Eat
Goose but was Denied this Delight by His Unfaithful Wife and Her Arrogant but
Probably Handsome Lover.*

A simple husband one morning took his wife a goose and said, Cook
this bird for me; when I come home in the evening I shall eat it.

The wife plucked the bird, cleaned it, and cooked it. In the afternoon
her lover came. Before going away he asked what food he could take
with him to his friends. He looked into the oven and saw the roasted
goose.

That is for my husband, the wife said.

I want it, the lover said. If you do not let me take it, I shall never love
you again.

The lover went off with the goose.

In the evening the husband sat at the table and said, Bring me the
goose.

What goose? the wife said.

The goose I brought you this morning, the husband said. Bring it to
me.

Are you serious? the wife said. You brought me no goose. Perhaps
you dreamed it.

Bring me the goose, the husband shouted.

The wife began to scream, saying, My poor husband has lost his mind.
My poor husband is crazy. What he has dreamed he imagines has happened.

The neighbors came and believed the wife, so the husband said nothing and went hungry, except for bread and cheese and water.

The following morning the husband brought his wife another goose
and said, Is this a goose?

Yes, the wife said.

Am I dreaming?—No.

Is this the goose's head?—Yes.

Wings?—Yes.

Feathers?—Yes.

All right, the husband said, cook it. When I come home tonight I'll eat it.

The wife cooked the goose. The lover came.

There is another goose today, he said. I can smell it.

You cannot take it, the wife said. I had a terrible scene with my husband last night, and again this morning. It is too much, I love you but you cannot have the goose.

Either you love me or you don't love me, the lover said. Either I take the goose or not.

So he took the goose.

Bring the goose, the husband said.

My poor husband, the wife screamed. He's stark raving mad. Goose, goose, goose. What goose? There is no goose. My poor, poor husband.

The neighbors came and again believed the wife.

The husband went hungry.

The following morning he bought another goose in the city. He hired a tall man to carry the goose on a platter on his head. He hired an orchestra of six pieces, and with the musicians in a circle around the tall man carrying the goose, he walked with them through the streets to his house, calling to his neighbors.

When he reached his house there were many people following him.

He turned to the people and said, Mohammedans, neighbors, the world, heaven above, fish in the sea, soldiers, and all others, behold, a goose.

He lifted the bird off the platter.

A goose, he cried.

He handed the bird to his wife.

Now cook the damned thing, he said, and when I come home in the evening I will eat it.

The wife cleaned the bird and cooked it. The lover came. There was a tender scene, tears, kisses, running, more tears, more kisses, and the lover went off with the goose.

In the city the husband saw an old friend and said, Come out to the house with me tonight; the wife's roasting a goose; we'll take a couple of bottles of *rakki* and have a hell of a time.

So the husband and his friend went out to the house and the husband said, Have you cooked the goose?

Yes, the wife said. It's in the oven.

Good, the husband said. You were never really a bad wife. First, my friend and I will have a few drinks: then we will eat the goose.

The husband and his friend had a few drinks and then the husband said, All right, bring the goose.

The wife said, There is no bread; go to your cousin's for bread; goose is no good without bread.

All right, the husband said.

He left the house.

The wife said to the husband's friend, My husband is crazy. There is no goose. He has brought you here to kill you with this enormous carving knife and this fork. You had better go.

The man went. The husband came home and asked about his friend and the goose.

Your *friend* has run off with the goose, the wife said. What kind of a friend do you call that, after I slave all day to cook you a decent meal?

The husband took the carving knife and the fork and began running down the street. At length in the distance he saw his friend running and he called out, Just a leg, my friend, that's all.

My God, the other said, he is truly crazy.

The friend began to run faster than ever. Soon the husband could run no more. He returned wearily to his home and wife. Once again he ate his bread and cheese. After this plain food he began to drink *rakki* again.

As he drank, the truth began to come to him little by little, as it does through alcohol.

When he was very drunk he knew all about everything. He got up and quietly whacked his wife across the room.

If your lover's got to have a goose every day, he said, you could have told me. Tomorrow I will bring *two* of them. I get hungry once in a while myself, you know.

THE GROWN-UP PROBLEM

Art Buchwald

There has been so much discussion about teen-age problems that the grown-up problem is practically being ignored. And yet if you pick up a newspaper, you realize grown-ups are responsible for some of the most serious problems this country has ever faced.

For example, 60 percent of all crime in the United States is committed by grown-ups.

The birth rate among grown-up women is four times that of teenagers.

The divorce rate is double.

The purchasing power of grown-ups almost exceeds that of teenagers.

Grown-ups are responsible for more daytime accidents than any other age group.

The source of these statistics is sociology Prof. Heinrich Applebaum, B.A., M.S., LL.D., Y.E.H., Y.E.H., Y.E.H., who told me in an exclusive interview that his studies showed grown-ups were drifting farther away from society all the time.

"The average grown-up," Prof. Applebaum said, "feels his children don't understand him. The more time he spends with them, the less they communicate with him. So the adult feels isolated, insecure, and misunderstood. In defense he seeks out other grown-ups who feel the same way he does. Pretty soon they form gangs, go to the theater together, hold cocktail parties and dances, and before you know it you have a complete breakdown of the family."

"Why do you think grown-ups are constantly rebelling against their children, Professor?"

"I guess it's an age-old old age problem. You have parents wanting to break away and yet not having the nerve to cut the ties completely.

Grown-ups are afraid to stand up to their children, so they rebel against society instead."

"Do you think teen-agers could in some way be responsible for the behavior of their parents?"

"I definitely do," the Professor said. "Grown-ups try to emulate teen-agers. They want to do exactly what teen-agers do, which is to drink, smoke, and drive fast cars. If teen-agers didn't do these things, their parents wouldn't. For every bad adult in America, I'm sure you'll find a bad teen-ager somewhere in the background."

"Where do you think the trouble starts?"

"In the home. Teen-agers are too rough on their parents. They're always criticizing them for listening to Frank Sinatra records and reading *Holiday* magazine. Teen-agers don't have any patience with their mothers and fathers. They can't understand why their parents like Doris Day and Rock Hudson movies or what they see in Cary Grant. If teen-agers spent more time with grown-ups and tried to understand them, I don't think you'd have half the trouble that you have in the United States today."

"Do you mean teen-agers should spend more time at home with their parents?"

"Of course. Grown-ups need security. They want to know where their children are. They want the feeling they belong. Only teen-agers can give grown-ups this feeling."

"Professor, have you found any homes where grown-ups are leading healthy, normal, secure lives, thanks to the attention they've received from their loving teen-age children?"

"We haven't yet. But we've been looking only a year. These surveys take time."

"It happens that neither of us is interested."

"Well, why not?"

HUMOR IN THE HEADLINES

DOCTOR COMPILES LIST OF POISONS CHILDREN MAY DRINK AT HOME

Buffalo (N.Y.) Times

SIX NEW FAMILIES TO BE CONNECTED TO SEWER

Clinton (Ok.) Morning Times

BOY, 14, BEATS WOMAN WITH PRIZE SPONGE CAKE

Madison (Wi.) Wisconsin State Journal

AVOID HAVING BABY AT DINNER TABLE

Minneapolis (Mn.) Daily Herald

TWO CONVICTS
EVADE NOOSE; JURY HUNG

Oakland (Ca.) Tribune

SALESMAN SAYS
HE LEFT 4 LARGE RINGS
IN MALDEN MOTEL BATHTUB

Malden (Mass.) News

NEW DUMB WAITER AT HOTEL

Wilkes-Barre (Pa.) Times Leader

CASE OF STOLEN WHISKEY
EXPECTED TO GO TO JURY

New Brunswick (N.J.) Sunday Home News

ILLINOIS MAN PULLS NEEDLE
FROM FOOT HE SWALLOWED 66 YEARS AGO

Greenville (Miss.) Daily Democrat Times

MANY NEW SHAPES
IN BATHTUBS THIS SEASON

San Francisco (Ca.) Examiner

"MISS WEST VIRGINIA"
IS HIT WITH ROTARY CLUB

Williamson (W.Va.) Daily News

REVOLTING DEMOCRATS BREAKFAST

Reno (Nevada) Gazette

MAN WITH TWO BROKEN LEGS SAVES
ONE FROM DROWNING

Pensacola (Fl.) News

FEEBLE-MINDED SCHOOL DEAN
HAS RESIGNED

Washington (Pa.) Observer

TOWN TO DROP SCHOOL BUS
WHEN OVERPASS IS READY

Providence (R.I.) Evening Bulletin

FARMER'S HORSES REPLACED BY CHURCH MEMBERS

New Bern (N.C.) Sun-Journal

DEAF MAN TO GET NEW HEARING IN COURT

Cincinnati (Ohio) Times-Star

DOPE JAILS TWO SAILORS

Pittsburgh (Pa.) Post-Gazette

DENIAL MADE BY TEACHER OF BRUTALITY

Dallas (Tex.) News

YOUNG DEMOCRATS ELECT BONE HEAD

Selma (Ala.) Times-Journal

A WAY
OF SEEING

GRAFFITI LIVES

Bonnie O'Boyle

The time is coming when maintenance men and cleaning women may be branded as book burners. Every day they go about their work scrubbing, mopping and obliterating the real nitty-gritty pop literature of our time: graffiti, the writing on the walls. The janitors of the world don't think of that as literature, but Edward Albee paid tribute to a question scribbled on a wall by using it as a play title: "Who's Afraid of Virginia Woolf?" And "Stop the World, I Want To Get Off" was a popular London graffito (singular of graffiti) long before it went up in lights advertising Anthony Newley's musical.

As literature, graffiti's conceits, ideas, splendid suspensions of logic and twisted aphorisms have turned up in the popular language of the people. Some graffiti properly belong in Bartlett's *Familiar Quotations,* like "God isn't dead, He's living in Argentina under an assumed name"; "Yankee, go home! And take me with you"; Stamp out mental health"; "Draft beer, not men." And if "Burn, baby, burn" didn't begin as a graffito, it had most of its exposure on walls.

A good graffito has all the qualities of an old saying or adage—it's short, memorable and has low-voltage shock quality. It often has humor, sometimes black humor with an unpleasant bite: "Ban the bomb, save the world for conventional warfare" is a famous New York underground statement that destroys some of your complacency. Other graffiti hark back to the Keystone cops type of slapstick, shriveling a person or point with an absurd kind of ridicule bordering on the burlesque: "J. Edgar Hoover sleeps with a night lite." The best humorous graffiti take a droll look at modern society and its hangups. An urban pessimist wrote "Chicken Little was right" on a pillar of New York's Lexington Avenue subway, for example. "Sacred cows make great hamburger" is not only a prime slice of wall-writing, it's a kind of manifesto of graffiti-dom. When the mammoth glass expanse of the Lever Building went up in New York, one anonymous person crouched ant-like in its shadow and chalked on the sidewalk, "In case of emergency, break glass and pull down lever." Everyone who feels like a pygmy in the cavernous American cities can appreciate the sentiment. On occasion, graffiti attack society—indirectly. For instance, couldn't "Mary Poppins is a junkie" be an admission that the world we live in isn't Disneyland after all?

Because wall-writing makes social comment and because it is spontaneous (or should be), sociologists, psychologists and historians are studying it seriously. This is a logical development. For some time, social scientists have been popularizing their disciplines by delving into studies of comic books, daytime serials and even motion picture fan clubs. Any contemporary development, they reason, fills a human need and therefore is a potential source of information about the humans involved. Wall-writing has even gone into the university classroom via a course taught at the New School for Social Research in New York by Robert Reisner, a jazz critic and humorist turned graffiti scholar (*Great Wall Writing* is one of his books). He doesn't consider it unusual that academicians are starting to analyze graffiti: "The question isn't why they're doing it now, but why people didn't notice wall-writing hundreds of years ago. Sometimes the humblest remains—like graffiti—are evidence of symptoms of society, but they're so apparent that people ignore them. Instead, studies were made about why gray-eyed people ate ham on Wednesdays. The historical graffiti tell us how common people lived, something you don't always find in history which comes down to us from the nobles' point of view. Today, too, the walls reflect what's happening. They show us that people are informed and that this is a sophisticated, cultured society."

The civil rights movement, for instance, is documented by graffiti. There are the scrawled slogans of the ghettos, from Watts to Harlem: "Black Power now" and "Burn, baby, burn." There are also the racist responses, like this one which cropped up on a New York campus: "All Negroes get out of City College." Reisner believes such remarks are valuable because they publicize issues that aren't honestly debated in the mass media, where they're written about in polite euphemisms. "A hate message doesn't mean that the whole country hates something," he says, "but just seeing such a statement is beneficial because otherwise we would feel that everything is rosy." A near-classic debate took place at Northwestern University after an Afro-American newspaper had been mutilated. Someone retaliated by writing "Black is beautiful" on a wall. That was scratched out and replaced with "White ain't so bad." Final word came the next night. "Black is *still* beautiful."

Graffiti dialogues are a form of free communication. The public writing place is an open forum for the writer and critics to carry on comparison and refutation. One of the classic graffiti sequences, a delightful exchange, started with the comment: "I like Grils." Underneath, a second person wrote: "It's girls, stupid, G-I-R-L-S." And a third passerby added the punch line: "What about us Grils?"

On the other hand, national causes can provoke real graffiti wars. Not long ago the perennial border dispute between the Irish Republic and Northern Ireland (still under the English crown) broke out again. Both sides made their positions clear on the walls of Belfast. The Northerners wrote "Up the Queen" and "No Pope here," while the Catholic Republicans scribbled back "No Queen here" and "Up the Pope," adding for good measure "Up Celtic" (the name of a Catholic Scottish soccer team).

The most ancient examples of graffiti are probably the scratchings found on early Egyptian monuments. Hieroglyphs also jump to mind as wall-writings, but these aren't true graffiti because they represent systematic accounts or stories rather than single statements. Graffiti, instead, are just what their name indicates—"scratches" or "scribbles" from the Italian verb *graffiare*.

In 1868, archeologists uncovered barracks used by the Seventh Battalion of the Roman police, and scratched on the walls were graffiti nearly two thousand years old, giving some very blunt, funny (sometimes obscene) views of the officers and the Roman emperors. Wall-writing must have been a widespread problem in ancient Rome. We know property owners near the Porta Portuensis had to put out a sign asking people not to scribble on their walls. The medieval knights had their coats of arms carved on churches to indicate their attendance for a ceremony or the end of a pilgrimage, and it isn't hard to see in these the forerunners of the initials carved in the old oak tree. Other ancient graffiti are less pleasant, like the words carved in the wall of Ashwell Church just as the Black Death was sweeping England in the fourteenth century: "The beginning of the plague was in 1350 minus one . . . wretched, fierce, violent." This staccato message conveys the atmosphere of the times in a flash.

Most graffiti are anonymous, but we know that sharp-tongued Jonathan Swift wrote this one on the window of an English inn called The Three Crosses: "There are three crosses at your door; hang up your wife and you'll count four." Public inns and houses provided most of the graffiti put into what was possibly the first collection ever made, a book called *"The Merry-Thought; or, the Glass-Window and Bog-House Miscellany"* which was published in England in 1731 by a man with the droll name of Hurlo Thrumbo. In his introduction, Thrumbo decried the careless destruction of casual scribblings, especially by the innkeeper, "his rooms new-painted and white-wash'd every now and then, without regarding in the least the Wit and Learning he is obliterating, or the Worthy Authors, any more than when he shall have their Company."

Why do people write on walls? To deface the property of an enemy, to shock passersby with obscenities, to express opinions and emotions, to pass the time? There are a lot of reasons. This was discovered by psychiatrist Harvey Lomas and his assistant Gershen Weltman when they scoured bars, hospitals, gas stations and schools in the Los Angeles area to prepare a recent graffiti report for the American Psychiatric Association. They found that some people even use graffiti as a way of roping off territory or proving themselves, like the boy who wrote "This is Tony's turf" on a wall. People carve their initials on walls, tables and telephone booths for the same reason—they want to put their names on something for posterity. Sometimes it's the only kind of possession an underprivileged person can have.

Initialing is also a traditional custom in certain spots, especially in favorite college social hubs, like Morey's at Yale, where undergraduates have been carving their initials on the tables for decades. Morey's has turned up in songs, poems and stories; it's even in *Frank Merriwell at Yale*, where a rival of Frank's is touted as "the most influential soph in college" because his initials were on a round table down at Morey's.

Psychiatry and tradition aside, there is one simple explanation for our walls being covered with graffiti—people want an audience for their wit, their frustrations, even their hates. Graffiti are free in every sense.

There are no editors, proofreaders, publishers, or typesetters to wade through, not even a censor until the janitor comes along. And if your graffito is in a subway or railroad station, it can stay up until the next paint job. Certainly there is a disproportionate amount of egotism involved in marking up somebody else's property with personal initials and sentiments like "*I* hate cops," "John [*I* the writer] loves Mary" and "Clancy [that *I* again] was here." Travelers on the London underground were mystified by a graffito in exotic script until it was identified by a scholar as Osmania (a written version of the Somali language) and translated: "*I* hate English pudding!"

Even the intellectual graffiti are at bottom hubris-ridden, a kind of showing off on a sophisticated level, but the results are so entertaining that it doesn't matter. One of the best thinking-man's graffiti was discovered in New York. The first line was: "Shakespeare eats Bacon" followed by: "It can't be Donne."

All meaningless unless you remember your English literature. The Ivy League colleges are noted for intellectual gamesmanship on their walls. The nerve center is Harvard's Lamont Library, which displays such classics as "Reality is a crutch," "War is good business. Invest your sons," and "God isn't dead. He just doesn't want to get involved." But the prize for inscrutability should go to Yale, where a student wrote in Japanese his opinion of a prominent architect: "Yamasaki is strictly Shinto Gothic." Yale also indirectly inspired a graffito that made the pages of the *New York Times*. After the University had released its map indicating that Leif Ericson, not Columbus, had discovered America, the *Times* ran (as its "Quotation of the Day") an opinion from Boston's Italian district: "Leif Ericson is a fink."

Anyone can write graffiti, but most come from the poor, who cover their neighborhoods, tunnels and underpasses with names, four-letter words and revolutionary slogans. Other great sources are the intellectual communities of Greenwich Village and Haight-Ashbury, who register their comments on the walls of coffeehouses. The middle-class masses probably make some contribution although Lomas and Weltman say they use "commercial graffiti" instead. Surprisingly, businessmen pick up cultural trends faster than sociologists at times. The commercial graffiti are the buttons and bumper stickers in neon colors that take their messages from the walls and are sold in book and card shops.

All the great graffiti like "Frodo lives" and "Help retard children—Support our schools" have ended up on buttons. Reisner calls the button phenomenon "walking graffiti": "They're used by people who are expressing a sentiment openly, not anonymously on the walls, but of course, it's not original. A lot of the people who buy those buttons don't even believe in what the message is—they just think it's a smart thing to do. Sometimes they even hide them under their lapels and flash them to friends that way."

Commercialization is one of the great compliments paid to contemporary graffiti. You can't market "Foxie was here" to the general public, but you can market today's imaginative mural output without worrying about authors' rights. Graffiti have never been better. Take the classic graffito of the World War II period, the ubiquitous "Kilroy was here," which isn't especially interesting and was drained of humor long ago. Today Kilroy has been replaced by a mysterious being called Overby who appears in what might be called metaphysical statements like "Overby lives" or "Overby rules." What is Overby? The Establishment perhaps, or even that other great enemy of American youth: "Down with the draft, Overby strikes every seven hours." Like much good literature, a graffito lends itself to interpretation.

Thrumbo's complaint is still unheeded after 238 years: landlords and keepers of public houses continue to whitewash graffiti. Yet no one has succeeded in stemming the flow. Certainly signs such as "Do not write on the walls" have no effect, except as inspiration for retorts like "Maybe we should type?" Which is just as well.

Graffiti

Do the Chinese Look
in the White Pages?
‡ ₤ ₣

I Claim This Wall for Queen Elizabeth

An Elephant is a Mouse
Drawn to Government
Specifications

Huckleberry Fim is a Dessert

the Scrawl of the Wild

The World is FLAT
Class of 1491

Help Stamp Out and Abolish Redundancy

I'm Neither For nor Against Apathy

Support Poetry or
I'll Kill You

RÉSUMÉ

Dorothy Parker

Razors pain you;
  Rivers are damp;
  Acids stain you;
  And drugs cause cramp.
  Guns aren't lawful;
  Nooses give;
  Gas smells awful;
  You might as well live.

CODA

Dorothy Parker

There's little in taking or giving,
  There's little in water or wine;
This living, this living, this living
  Was never a project of mine.
Oh, hard is the struggle, and sparse is
  The gain of the one at the top,
For art is a form of catharsis,
  And love is a permanent flop,
And work is the province of cattle,
  And rest's for a clam in a shell,
So I'm thinking of throwing the battle—
  Would you kindly direct me to hell?

THE DEVIL'S DICTIONARY

Ambrose Bierce

ABSURDITY, *n.*   A statement or belief manifestly inconsistent with one's own opinion.

ADMIRATION, *n.*   Our polite recognition of another's resemblance to ourselves.

APOLOGIZE, *v.i.*   To lay the foundation for a future offense.

BORE, *n.*   A person who talks when you wish him to listen.

CONGRATULATION, *n,*   The civility of envy.

EPITAPH, *n.*   An inscription on a tomb, showing that virtues acquired by death have a retroactive effect.

FRIENDLESS, *adj.*   Having no favors to bestow. Destitute of fortune. Addicted to utterance of truth and common sense.

HOSPITALITY, *n.*   The virtue which induces us to feed and lodge certain persons who are not in need of food and lodging.

LOVE,   *n.*   A temporary insanity curable by marriage or by removal of the patient from the influences under which he incurred the disorder. This disease, like caries and many other ailments, is prevalent only among civilized races living under artificial conditions; barbarous nations breathing pure air and eating simple food enjoy immunity from its ravages. It is sometimes fatal, but more frequently to the physician than to the patient.

MAN,   *n.*   An animal so lost in rapturous contemplation of what he thinks he is as to overlook what he indubitably ought to be. His chief occupation is extermination of other animals and his own species, which, however, multiplies with such insistent rapidity as to infest the whole habitable earth.

PATIENCE,   *n.*   A minor form of despair, disguised as a virtue.

POLITICS,   *n.*   A strife of interests masquerading as a contest of principles. The conduct of public affairs for private advantage.

POSITIVE,   *adj.*   Mistaken at the top of one's voice.

TWICE,   *adj.*   Once too often.

UN-AMERICAN,   *adj.*   Wicked, intolerable, heathenish.

WAR,   *n.*   A by-product of the arts of peace.

CLASSIC PUT-DOWNS

Selected by
Bergen Evans

An impertinent young man, belittling literature in Samuel Johnson's presence, asserted that a good cook was worth all the writers in the world. "And in that opinion, Sir," Johnson said sternly, "you have the support of *every* dog in town."

Of a certain savant Voltaire remarked, "He is tremendously ignorant; he can answer any question put to him."

"If Mr. Gladstone fell into the Thames, that would be a misfortune. If someone fished him out, that would be a calamity."

[Attributed to Benjamin Disraeli, when asked what the difference was between a *misfortune* and a *calamity*. Under the jesting there was a sincere dislike. Disraeli once referred to Gladstone as "a sophistical rhetorician, inebriated with the exuberance of his own verbosity."]

"The Right Honorable gentleman is indebted to his memory for his jests and to his imagination for his facts."

Richard Brinsley Sheridan

"He has a great deal to be modest about!"

[Sir Winston Churchill's retort to one who stated that
Clement Atlee (whom Churchill disliked) was a modest man.]

"Winston, if you were my husband, I'd put poison in your coffee!"

"Nancy, if you were my wife, I'd drink it."

[Reputed exchange between Sir Winston Churchill
and Lady Nancy Astor]

The great English playwright George Bernard Shaw was also
known as a great wit. He cabled the following invitation
to Sir Winston Churchill:

HAVE RESERVED TWO TICKETS FOR MY FIRST NIGHT.
COME AND BRING A FRIEND, IF YOU HAVE ONE.

SHAW

Churchill, however, had the final word when he replied:

IMPOSSIBLE TO COME TO FIRST NIGHT. WILL COME
TO SECOND NIGHT, IF YOU HAVE ONE.

CHURCHILL

Charles Chaplin in *Modern Times*

Harold Lloyd in *Safety Last*

COMEDY'S GREATEST ERA

James Agee

In the language of screen comedians four of the main grades of laugh are the titter, the yowl, the bellylaugh and the boffo. The titter is just a titter. The yowl is a runaway titter. Anyone who has ever had the pleasure knows all about a bellylaugh. The boffo is the laugh that kills. An ideally good gag, perfectly constructed and played, would bring the victim up this ladder of laughs by cruelly controlled degrees to the top rung, and would then proceed to wobble, shake, wave and brandish the ladder until he groaned for mercy. Then, after the shortest possible time out for recuperation, he would feel the first wicked tickling of the comedian's whip once more and start up a new ladder.

The reader can get a fair enough idea of the current state of screen comedy by asking himself how long it has been since he has had that treatment. The best of comedies these days hand out plenty of titters and once in a while it is possible to achieve a yowl without overstraining. Even those who have never seen anything better must occasionally have the feeling, as they watch the current run or, rather, trickle of screen comedy, that they are having to make a little cause for laughter go an awfully long way. And anyone who has watched screen comedy over the past ten or fifteen years is bound to realize that it has quietly but steadily deteriorated. As for those happy atavists who remember silent comedy in its heyday and the bellylaughs and boffos that went with it, they have something close to an absolute standard by which to measure the deterioration.

When a modern comedian gets hit on the head, for example, the most he is apt to do is look sleepy. When a silent comedian got hit on the head he seldom let it go so flatly. He realized a broad license, and a ruthless discipline within that license. It was his business to be as funny as possible physically, without the help or hindrance of words. So he gave us a figure of speech, or rather of vision, for loss of consciousness. In other words he gave us a poem, a kind of poem, moreover, that everybody understands. The least he might do was to straighten up stiff as a plank and fall over backward with such skill that his whole length seemed to slap the floor at the same instant. Or he might make a cadenza of it— look vague, smile like an angel, roll up his eyes, lace his fingers, thrust his hands palms downward as far as they would go, hunch his shoulders, rise on tiptoe, prance ecstatically in narrowing circles until, with tallow knees, he sank down the vortex of his dizziness to the floor, and there signified nirvana by kicking his heels twice, like a swimming frog.

Startled by a cop, this same comedian might grab his hatbrim with both hands and yank it down over his ears, jump high in the air, come to earth in a split violent enough to telescope his spine, spring thence into a coattail-flattening sprint and dwindle at rocket speed to the size of a gnat along the grand, forlorn perspective of some lazy back boulevard.

Those are fine clichés from the language of silent comedy in its infancy. The man who could handle them properly combined several of the more difficult accomplishments of the acrobat, the dancer, the clown and the mime. Some very gifted comedians, unforgettably Ben Turpin, had an immense vocabulary of these clichés and were in part so lovable because they were deep conservative classicists and never tried to break away from them. The still more gifted men, of course, simplified and invented, finding out new and much deeper uses for the idiom. They learned to show emotion through it, and comic psychology, more eloquently than most language has ever managed to, and they discovered beauties of comic motion which are hopelessly beyond reach of words.

It is hard to find a theater these days where a comedy is playing; in the days of the silents it was equally hard to find a theater which was not showing one. The laughs today are pitifully few, far between, shallow, quiet and short. They almost never build, as they used to, into something combining the jabbering frequency of a machine gun with the delirious momentum of a roller coaster. Saddest of all, there are few comedians now below middle age and there are none who seem to learn much from picture to picture, or to try anything new.

To put it unkindly, the only thing wrong with screen comedy today is that it takes place on a screen which talks. Because it talks, the only comedians who ever mastered the screen cannot work, for they cannot combine their comic style with talk. Because there is a screen, talking comedians are trapped into a continual exhibition of their inadequacy as screen comedians on a surface as big as the side of a barn.

At the moment, as for many years past, the chances to see silent comedy are rare. There is a smattering of it on television—too often treated as something quaintly archaic, to be laughed at, not with. Some two hundred comedies—long and short—can be rented for home projection. And a lucky minority has access to the comedies in the collection of New York's Museum of Modern Art, which is still incomplete but which is probably the best in the world. In the near future, however, something of this lost art will return to regular theaters. A thick straw in the wind is the big business now being done by a series of revivals of W.C. Fields's memorable movies, a kind of comedy more akin to the old silent variety than anything which is being made today. Mack Sennett now is preparing a sort of pot-pourri variety show called *Down Memory Lane* made up out of his old movies, featuring people like Fields and Bing Crosby when they were movie beginners, but including also interludes from silents. Harold Lloyd has re-released *Movie Crazy,* a talkie, and plans to revive four of his best silent comedies (*Grandma's Boy, Safety Last, Speedy* and *The Freshman*). Buster Keaton hopes to remake at feature length, with a minimum of dialogue, two of the funniest short comedies ever made, one about a porous homemade boat and one about a prefabricated house.

Awaiting these happy events we will discuss here what has gone wrong with screen comedy and what, if anything, can be done about it. But mainly we will try to suggest what it was like in its glory in the years from 1912 to 1930, as practiced by the employees of Mack Sennett, the father of American screen comedy, and by the four most eminent masters: Charlie Chaplin, Harold Lloyd, the late Harry Langdon and Buster Keaton.

Mack Sennett made two kinds of comedy: parody laced with slapstick, and plain slapstick. The parodies were the unceremonious burial of a century of hamming, including the new hamming in serious movies, and nobody who has missed Ben Turpin in A *Small Town Idol,* or kidding Erich von Stroheim in *Three Foolish Weeks* or as *The Shriek of Araby,* can imagine how rough parody can get and still remain subtle and roaringly funny. The plain slapstick, at its best, was even better: a profusion of hearty young women in disconcerting bathing suits, frisking around with a gaggle of insanely incompetent policemen and of equally certifiable male civilians sporting museum-piece mustaches. All these people zipped and caromed about the pristine world of the screen as jazzily as a convention of water bugs. Words can hardly suggest how energetically they collided and bounced apart, meeting in full gallop around the corner of a house; how hard and how often they fell on their backsides; or with what fantastically adroit clumsiness they got themselves fouled up in folding ladders, garden hoses, tethered animals and each other's headlong cross-purposes. The gestures were ferociously emphatic; not a line or motion of the body was wasted or inarticulate. The reader may remember how splendidly upright wandlike old Ben Turpin could stand for a Renunciation Scene, with his lampshade mustache twittering and his sparrowy chest stuck out and his head flung back like Paderewski assaulting a climax and the long babyish back hair trying to look lionlike, while his Adam's apple, an orange in a Christmas stocking, pumped with noble emotion. Or huge Mack Swain, who looked like a hairy mushroom, rolling his eyes in a manner patented by French Romantics and gasping in some dubious ecstasy. Or Louise Fazenda, the perennial farmer's daughter and the perfect low-comedy housemaid, primping her spit curl; and how her hair tightened a good-looking face into the incarnation of rampant gullibility. Or snouty James Finlayson, gleefully foreclosing a mortgage, with his look of eternally tasting a spoiled pickle. Or Chester Conklin, a myopic and inebriated little walrus stumbling around in outsize pants. Or Fatty Arbuckle, with his cold eye and his loose, serene smile, his silky manipulation of his bulk and his satanic marksmanship with pies (he was ambidextrous and could simultaneously blind two people in opposite directions).

The intimate tastes and secret hopes of these poor ineligible dunces were ruthlessly exposed whenever a hot stove, an electric fan or a bulldog took a dislike to their outer garments: agonizingly elaborate drawers, worked up on some lonely evening out of some Godforsaken lace curtain; or men's underpants with big round black spots on them. The Sennett sets—delirious wall-paper, megalomaniacally scrolled iron beds, Grand Rapids *in extremis*—outdid even the underwear. It was their business, after all, to kid the squalid braggadocio which infested the domestic interiors of the period, and that was almost beyond parody. These comedies told their stories to the unaided eye, and by every means possible they screamed to it. That is one reason for the India-ink silhouettes of the cops, and for convicts and prison bars and their shadows in hard sunlight, and for barefooted husbands, in tigerish pajamas, reacting like dervishes to stepped-on tacks.

The early silent comedians never strove for or consciously thought of anything which could be called artistic "form," but they achieved it. For Sennett's rival, Hal Roach, Leo McCarey once devoted almost the whole of a Laurel and Hardy two-reeler to pie-throwing. The first pies were thrown thoughtfully, almost philosophically. Then innocent bystanders began to get caught into the vortex. At full pitch it was Armageddon. But everything was calculated so nicely that until late in the picture, when havoc took over, every pie made its special kind of point and piled on its special kind of laugh.

Sennett's comedies were just a shade faster and fizzier than life. According to legend (and according to Sennett) he discovered the speed tempo proper to screen comedy when a green cameraman, trying to save money, cranked too slow.* Realizing the tremendous drumlike power of mere motion to exhilarate, he gave inanimate objects a mischievous life of their own, broke every law of nature the tricked camera would serve him for and made the screen dance like a witches' Sabbath. The thing one is surest of all to remember is how toward the end of nearly every Sennett comedy, a chase (usually called the "rally") built up such a majestic trajectory of pure anarchic motion that bathing girls, cops, comics, dogs, cats, babies, automobiles, locomotives, innocent bystanders, sometimes what seemed like a whole city, an entire civilization, were hauled along head over heels in the wake of that energy like dry leaves following an express train.

"Nice" people, who shunned all movies in the early days, condemned the Sennett comedies as vulgar and naive. But millions of less pretentious people loved their sincerity and sweetness, their wild-animal innocence and glorious vitality. They could not put these feelings into words, but

---

*Silent comedy was shot at 12 to 16 frames per second and was speeded up by being shown at 16 frames per second, the usual rate of theater projectors at that time. Theater projectors today run at 24, which makes modern film taken at the same speed seem smooth and natural. But it makes silent movies fast and jerky.

they flocked to the silents. The reader who gets back deep enough into that world will probably even remember the theater: the barefaced honky-tonk and the waltzes by Waldteufel, slammed out on a mechanical piano; the searing redolence of peanuts and demirep perfumery, tobacco and feet and sweat; the laughter of unrespectable people having a hell of a fine time, laughter as violent and steady and deafening as standing under a waterfall.

Sennett wheedled his first financing out of a couple of ex-bookies to whom he was already in debt. He took his comics out of music halls, burlesque, vaudeville, circuses and limbo, and through them he tapped in on that great pipeline of horsing and miming which runs back unbroken through the fairs of the Middle Ages at least to ancient Greece. He added all that he himself had learned about the large and spurious gesture, the late decadence of the Grand Manner, as a stage-struck boy in East Berlin, Connecticut, and as a frustrated opera singer and actor. The only thing he claims to have invented is the pie in the face, and he insists, "Anyone who tells you he has discovered something new is a fool or a liar or both."

The silent-comedy studio was about the best training school the movies had ever known, and the Sennett studio was about as free and easy and as fecund of talent as they came. All the major comedians we will mention worked there, at least briefly. So did some of the major stars of the twenties and since—notably Gloria Swanson, Phyllis Haver, Wallace Beery, Marie Dressler and Carole Lombard. Directors Frank Capra, Leo McCarey and George Stevens also got their start in silent comedy; much that remains most flexible, spontaneous and visually alive in sound movies can be traced, through them and others, to this silent apprenticeship. Everybody did pretty much as he pleased on the Sennett lot, and everybody's ideas were welcome. Sennett posted no rules, and the only thing he strictly forbade was liquor. A Sennett story conference was a most informal affair. During the early years, at least, only the most important scenario might be jotted on the back of an envelope. Mainly Sennett's men thrashed out a few primary ideas and carried them in their heads, sure the better stuff would turn up while they were shooting, in the heat of physical action. This put quite a load on the prop man; he had to have the most improbable apparatus on hand— bombs, trick telephones, what not—to implement whatever idea might suddenly turn up. All kinds of things did—and were recklessly used. Once a low-comedy auto got out of control and killed the cameraman, but he was not visible in the shot, which was thrilling and undamaged; the audience never knew the difference.

Sennett used to hire a "wild man" to sit in on his gag conferences, whose whole job was to think up "wildies." Usually he was an all but brainless, speechless man, scarcely able to communicate his idea; but he had a totally uninhibited imagination. He might say nothing for an hour; then he'd mutter "You take . . ." and all the relatively rational others would shut up and wait. "You take this cloud . . ." he would get out, sketching vague shapes in the air. Often he could get no further; but thanks to some kind of thought-transference, saner men would take this cloud and make something of it. The wild man seems in fact to have functioned as the group's subconscious mind, the source of all creative energy. His ideas were so weird and amorphous that Sennett can no longer remember a one of them, or even how it turned out after rational processing. But a fair equivalent might be one of the best comic sequences in a Laurel and Hardy picture. It is simple enough—simple and real, in fact, as a nightmare. Laurel and Hardy are trying to move a piano across a narrow suspension bridge. The bridge is slung over a sickening chasm, between a couple of Alps. Midway they meet a gorilla.

Had he done nothing else, Sennett would be remembered for giving a start to three of the four comedians who now began to apply their sharp individual talents to this newborn language. The one whom he did not train (he was on the lot briefly but Sennett barely remembers seeing him around) wore glasses, smiled a great deal and looked like the sort of eager young man who might have quit divinity school to hustle brushes. That was Harold Lloyd. The others were grotesque and poetic in their screen characters in degrees which appear to be impossible when the magic of silence is broken. One, who never smiled, carried a face as still and sad as a daguerreotype through some of the most preposterously ingenious and visually satisfying physical comedy ever invented. That was Buster Keaton. One looked like an elderly baby and, at times, a baby dope fiend; he could do more with less than any other comedian. That was Harry Langdon. One looked like Charlie Chaplin, and he was the first man to give the silent language a soul.

When Charlie Chaplin started to work for Sennett he had chiefly to reckon with Ford Sterling, the reigning comedian. Their first picture together amounted to a duel before the assembled professionals. Sterling, by no means untalented, was a big man with a florid Teutonic style which, under this special pressure, he turned on full blast. Chaplin defeated him within a few minutes with a wink of the mustache, a hitch of the trousers, a quirk of the little finger.

With *Tillie's Punctured Romance,* in 1914, he became a major star. Soon after, he left Sennett when Sennett refused to start a landslide among the other comedians by meeting the raise Chaplin demanded. Sennett is understandably wry about it in retrospect, but he still says, "I was right at the time." Of Chaplin he says simply, "Oh well, he's just the greatest artist that ever lived." None of Chaplin's former rivals rate him much lower than that; they speak of him no more jealously than they might of God. We will try here only to suggest the essence of his supremacy. Of all comedians he worked most deeply and most shrewdly within a realization of what a human being is, and is up against. The Tramp is as centrally representative of humanity, as many-sided and as mysterious, as Hamlet, and it seems unlikely that any dancer or actor can ever have excelled him in eloquence, variety or poignancy of motion. As for pure motion, even if he had never gone on to make his magnificent feature-length comedies, Chaplin would have made his period in movies a great one single-handed even if he had made nothing except *The Cure,* or *One A.M.* In the latter, barring one immobile taxi driver, Chaplin plays alone, as a drunk trying to get upstairs and into bed. It is a sort of inspired elaboration on a soft-shoe dance, involving an angry stuffed wildcat, small rugs on slippery floors, a Lazy Susan table, exquisite footwork on a flight of stairs, a contretemps with a huge, ferocious pendulum and the funniest and most perverse Murphy bed in movie history—and, always made physically lucid, the delicately weird mental processes of a man ethereally sozzled.

Before Chaplin came to pictures people were content with a couple of gags per comedy; he got some kind of laugh every second. The minute he began to work he set standards—and continually forced them higher. Anyone who saw Chaplin eating a boiled shoe like brook trout in *The Gold Rush,* or embarrassed by a swallowed whistle in *City lights,* has seen perfection. Most of the time, however, Chaplin got his laughter less from the gags, or from milking them in any ordinary sense, than through his genius for what may be called *inflection*—the perfect, changeful shading of his physical and emotional attitudes toward the gag. Funny as his bout with the Murphy bed is, the glances of awe, expostulation and helpless, almost whimpering desire for vengeance which he darts at this infernal machine are even better.

A painful and frequent error among tyros is breaking the comic line with a too-big laugh, then a letdown; or with a laugh which is out of key or irrelevant. The masters could ornament the main line beautifully; they never addled it. In *A Night Out* Chaplin, passed out, is hauled along the sidewalk by the scruff of his coat by staggering Ben Turpin. His toes trail; he is as supine as a sled. Turpin himself is so drunk he can hardly drag him. Chaplin comes quietly to, realizes how well he is being served by his struggling pal, and with a royally delicate gesture plucks and savors a flower.

The finest pantomime, the deepest emotion, the richest and most poignant poetry were in Chaplin's work. He could probably pantomime Bryce's *The American Commonwealth* without ever blurring a syllable and make it paralyzingly funny into the bargain. At the end of *City Lights* the blind girl who has regained her sight, thanks to the Tramp, sees him for the first time. She has imagined and anticipated him as princely, to say the least; and it has never seriously occurred to him that he is inadequate. She recognizes who he must be by his shy, confident, shining joy as he comes silently toward her. And he recognizes himself, for the first time, through the terrible changes in her face. The camera just exchanges a few quiet close-ups of the emotions which shift and intensify in each face. It is enough to shrivel the heart to see, and it is the greatest piece of acting and the highest moment in movies.

Harold Lloyd worked only a little while with Sennett. During most of his career he acted for another major comedy producer, Hal Roach. He tried at first to offset Chaplin's influence and establish his own individuality by playing Chaplin's exact opposite, a character named Lonesome Luke who wore clothes much too small for him and whose gestures were likewise as unChaplinesque as possible. But he soon realized that an opposite in itself was a kind of slavishness. He discovered his own comic identity when he saw a movie about a fighting parson: a hero who wore glasses. He began to think about those glasses day and night. He decided on horn rims because they were youthful, ultravisible on the screen and on the verge of becoming fashionable (he was to make them so). Around these large lensless horn rims he began to develop a new character, nothing grotesque or eccentric, but a fresh, believable young man who could fit into a wide variety of stories.

Lloyd depended more on story and situation than any of the other major comedians (he kept the best stable of gagmen in Hollywood, at one time hiring six); but unlike most "story" comedians he was also a very funny man from inside. He had, as he has written, "an unusually large comic vocabulary." More particularly he had an expertly expressive body and even more expressive teeth, and out of his thesaurus of smiles he could at a moment's notice blend prissiness, breeziness and asininity, and still remain tremendously likable. His movies were more extroverted and closer to ordinary life than any others of the best comedies: the vicissitudes of a New York taxi driver; the unaccepted college boy who, by desperate courage and inspired ineptitude, wins the Big Game. He was especially good at putting a very timid, spoiled or brassy young fellow through devastating embarrassments. He went through one of his most uproarious Gethsemanes as a shy country youth courting the nicest girl in town in *Grandma's Boy*. He arrived dressed "strictly up to date for the Spring of 1862," as a subtitle observed, and found that the ancient colored butler wore a similar flowered waistcoat and moldering cutaway. He got one wandering, nervous forefinger dreadfully stuck in a fancy little vase. The girl began cheerfully to try to identify that queer smell which dilated from him; Grandpa's best suit was rife with mothballs. A tenacious litter of kittens feasted off the goose grease on his home-shined shoes.

Lloyd was even better at the comedy of thrills. In *Safety Last,* as a rank amateur, he is forced to substitute for a human fly and to climb a medium-sized skyscraper. Dozens of awful things happen to him. He gets fouled up in a tennis set. Popcorn falls on him from a window above, and the local pigeons treat him like a cross between a lunch wagon and St. Francis of Assisi. A mouse runs up his britches-leg, and the crowd below salutes his desperate dance on the window ledge with wild applause of the daredevil. A good deal of this full-length picture hangs thus by its eyelashes along the face of a building. Each new floor is like a new stanza in a poem; and the higher and more horrifying it gets, the funnier it gets.

In this movie Lloyd demonstrates beautifully his ability to do more than merely milk a gag, but to top it. (In an old, simple example of topping, an incredible number of tall men get, one by one, out of a small closed auto. After as many have clambered out as the joke will bear, one more steps out: a midget. That tops the gag. Then the auto collapses. That tops the topper.) In *Safety Last* Lloyd is driven out to the dirty end of a flagpole by a furious dog; the pole breaks and he falls, just managing to grab the minute hand of a huge clock. His weight promptly pulls the hand down from IX to VI. That would be more than enough for any ordinary comedian, but there is further logic in the situation. Now, hideously, the whole clockface pulls loose and slants from its trembling springs above the street. Getting out of difficulty with the clock, he makes still further use of the instrument by getting one foot caught in one of these obstinate springs.

A proper delaying of the ultrapredictable can of course be just as funny as a properly timed explosion of the unexpected. As Lloyd approaches the end of his horrible hegira up the side of the building in *Safety Last*, it becomes clear to the audience, but not to him, that if he raises his head another couple of inches he is going to get murderously conked by one of the four arms of a revolving wind gauge. He delays the evil moment almost interminably, with one distraction and another, and every delay is a suspense-tightening laugh; he also gets his foot nicely entangled in a rope, so that when he does get hit, the payoff of one gag sends him careening head downward through the abyss into another. Lloyd was outstanding even among the master craftsmen at setting up a gag clearly, culminating and getting out of it deftly, and linking it smoothly to the next. Harsh experience also taught him a deep and fundamental rule: never try to get "above" the audience.

Lloyd tried it in *The Freshman*. He was to wear an unfinished, basted-together tuxedo to a college party, and it would gradually fall apart as he danced. Lloyd decided to skip the pants, a low-comedy cliché, and lose just the coat. His gagmen warned him. A preview proved how right they were. Lloyd had to reshoot the whole expensive sequence, build it around defective pants and climax it with the inevitable. It was one of the funniest things he ever did.

When Lloyd was still a very young man he lost about half his right hand (and nearly lost his sight) when a comedy bomb exploded prematurely. But in spite of his artificially built-out hand he continued to do his own dirty work, like all of the best comedians. The side of the building he climbed in *Safety Last* did not overhang the street, as it appears to. But the nearest landing place was a roof three floors below him, as he approached the top, and he did everything, of course, the hard way, that is, the comic way, keeping his bottom stuck well out, his shoulders hunched, his hands and feet skidding over perdition.

If great comedy must involve something beyond laughter, Lloyd was not a great comedian. If plain laughter is any criterion—and it is a healthy counterbalance to the other—few people have equaled him, and nobody has ever beaten him.

Chaplin and Keaton and Lloyd were all more like each other, in one important way, than Harry Langdon was like any of them. Whatever else the others might be doing, they all used more or less elaborate physical comedy; Langdon showed how little of that one might use and still be a great silent-screen comedian. In his screen character he symbolized something as deeply and centrally human, though by no means as rangily so, as the Tramp. There was, of course, an immense difference in inventiveness and range of virtuosity. It seemed as if Chaplin could do literally anything, on any instrument in the orchestra. Langdon had one queerly toned, unique little reed. But out of it he could get incredible melodies.

Like Chaplin, Langdon wore a coat which buttoned on his wishbone and swung out wide below, but the effect was very different: he seemed like an outsized baby who had begun to outgrow his clothes. The crown of his hat was rounded and the brim was turned up all around, like a little boy's hat, and he looked as if he wore diapers under his pants. His walk was that of a child which has just gotten sure on its feet, and his body and hands fitted that age. His face was kept pale to show off, with the simplicity of a nursery-school drawing, the bright, ignorant, gentle eyes and the little twirling mouth. He had big moon cheeks, with dimples, and a Napoleonic forelock of mousy hair; the round, docile head seemed large in ratio to the cream-puff body. Twitchings of his face were signals of tiny discomforts too slowly registered by a tinier brain; quick squirty little smiles showed his almost prehuman pleasures, his incurably premature truthfulness. He was a virtuoso of hesitations and of delicately indecisive motions, and he was particularly fine in a high wind, rounding a corner with a kind of skittering toddle, both hands nursing his hatbrim.

He was as remarkable a master as Chaplin of subtle emotional and mental process and operated much more at leisure. He once got a good three hundred feet of continously bigger laughs out of rubbing his chest, in a crowded vehicle, with Limburger cheese, under the misapprehension that it was a cold salve. In another long scene, watching a brazen showgirl change her clothes, he sat motionless, back to the camera, and registered the whole lexicon of lost innocence, shock, disapproval and disgust, with the back of his neck. His scenes with women were nearly always something special. Once a lady spy did everything in her power (under the Hays Office) to seduce him. Harry was polite, willing, even flirtatious in his little way. The only trouble was that he couldn't imagine what in the world she was leering and pawing at him for, and that he was terribly ticklish. The Mata Hari wound up foaming at the mouth.

There was also a sinister flicker of depravity about the Langdon character, all the more disturbing because babies are premoral. He had an instinct for bringing his actual adulthood and figurative babyishness into frictions as crawley as a fingernail on a slate blackboard, and he wandered into areas of strangeness which were beyond the other comedians. In a nightmare in one movie he was forced to fight a large, muscular young man; the girl Harry loved was the prize. The young man was a good boxer; Harry could scarcely lift his gloves. The contest took place in a fiercely lighted prize ring, in a prodigious pitch-dark arena. The only spectator was the girl, and she was rooting against Harry. As the fight went on, her eyes glittered ever more brightly with blood lust and, with glittering teeth, she tore her big straw hat to sheds.

Langdon came to Sennett from a vaudeville act in which he had fought a losing battle with a recalcitrant automobile. The minute Frank Capra saw him he begged Sennett to let him work with him. Langdon was almost as childlike as the character he played. He had only a vague idea of his story or even of each scene as he played it; each time he went before the camera Capra would brief him on the general situation and then, as this finest of intuitive improvisers once tried to explain his work, "I'd go into my routine." The whole tragedy of the coming of dialogue, as far as these comedians were concerned—and one reason for the increasing rigidity of comedy ever since—can be epitomized in the mere thought of Harry Landgon confronted with a script.

Langdon's magic was in his innocence, and Capra took beautiful care not to meddle with it. The key to the proper use of Langdon, Capra always knew, was "the principle of the brick." "If there was a rule for writing Langdon material," he explains, "it was this: his only ally was God. Langdon might be saved by the brick falling on the cop, but it was *verboten* that he in any way motivate the brick's fall." Langdon became quickly and fantastically popular with three pictures, *Tramp, Tramp, Tramp, The Strong Man* and *Long Pants;* from then on he went downhill even faster. "The trouble was," Capra says, "that high-brow critics came around to explain his art to him. Also he developed an interest in dames. It was a pretty high life for such a little fellow." Langdon made two more pictures with high-brow writers, one of which (*Three's A Crowd*) had some wonderful passages in it, including the prize-ring nightmare; then First National canceled his contract. He was reduced to mediocre roles and two-reelers which were more rehashes of his old gags; this time around they no longer seemed funny. "He never did really understand what hit him," says Capra. "He died broke [in 1944]. And he died of a broken heart. He was the most tragic figure I ever came across in show business."

Buster Keaton started work at the age of three and one-half with his parents in one of the roughest acts in vaudeville ("The Three Keatons"); Harry Houdini gave the child the name Buster in admiration for a fall he took down a flight of stairs. In his first movies Keaton teamed with Fatty Arbuckle under Sennett. He went on to become one of Metro's biggest stars and earners; a Keaton feature cost about $200,000 to make and reliably grossed $2,000,000. Very early in his movie career friends asked him why he never smiled on the screen. He didn't realize he didn't. He had got the dead-pan habit in variety; on the screen he had merely been so hard at work it had never occurred to him there was anything to smile about. Now he tried it just once and never again. He was by his whole style and nature so much the most deeply "silent" of the silent comedians that even a smile was as deafeningly out of key as a yell. In a way his pictures are like a transcendent juggling act in which it seems that the whole universe is in exquisite flying motion and the one point of repose is the juggler's effortless, uninterested face.

Keaton's face ranked almost with Lincoln's as an early American archetype; it was haunting, handsome, almost beautiful, yet it was irreducibly funny; he improved matters by topping it off with a deadly horizontal hat, as flat and thin as a phonograph record. One can never forget Keaton wearing it, standing erect at the prow as his little boat is being launched. The boat goes grandly down the skids and, just as grandly, straight on to the bottom. Keaton never budges. The last you see of him, the water lifts the hat off the stoic head and it floats away.

No other comedian could do as much with the dead pan. He used this great, sad, motionless face to suggest various related things: a one-track mind near the track's end of pure insanity; mulish imperturbability under the wildest of circumstances; how dead a human being can get and still be alive; an awe-inspiring sort of patience and power to endure, proper to granite but uncanny in flesh and blood. Everything that he was and did bore out this rigid face and played laughs against it. When he moved his eyes, it was like seeing them move in a statue. His short-legged body was all sudden, machinelike angles, governed by a daft aplomb. When he swept a semaphorelike arm to point, you could almost hear the electrical impulse in the signal block. When he ran from a cop, his transitions from accelerating walk to easy jogtrot to brisk canter to headlong gallop to flogged-piston sprint—always floating, above this frenzy, the untroubled, untouchable face—were as distinct and as soberly in order as an automatic gearshift.

Keaton was a wonderfully resourceful inventor of mechanistic gags (he still spends much of his time fooling with Erector sets); as he ran afoul of locomotives, steamships, prefabricated and over-electrified houses, he put himself through some of the hardest and cleverest punishment ever designed for laughs. In *Sherlock Jr.,* boiling along on the handlebars of a motorcycle quite unaware that he has lost his driver, Keaton whips through city traffic, breaks up a tug-of-war, gets a shovelful of dirt in the face from each of a long line of Rockette-timed ditch-diggers, approaches a log at high speed which is hinged open by dynamite precisely soon enough to let him through and, hitting an obstruction, leaves the handlebars like an arrow leaving a bow, whams through the window of a shack in which the heroine is about to be violated, and hits the heavy feet-first, knocking him through the opposite wall. The whole sequence is as clean in motion as the trajectory of a bullet.

Much of the charm and edge of Keaton's comedy, however, lay in the subtle leverages of expression he could work against his nominal dead pan. Trapped in the side-wheel of a ferryboat, saving himself from drowning only by walking, then desperately running, inside the accelerating wheel like a squirrel in a cage, his only real concern was, obviously, to keep his hat on. Confronted by Love, he was not as dead-pan as he was cracked up to be, either; there was odd, abrupt motion of his head which suggested a horse nipping after a sugar lump.

Keaton worked strictly for laughs, but work came from so far inside a curious and original spirit that he achieved a great deal besides, especially in his feature-length comedies. (For plain hard laughter his nineteen short comedies—the negatives of which have been lost—were even better.) He was the only major comedian who kept sentiment almost entirely out of his work, and he brought pure physical comedy to its greatest heights. Beneath his lack of emotion he was also uninsistently sardonic; deep below that, giving a disturbing tension and grandeur to the foolishness, for those who sensed it, there was in his comedy a freezing whisper not of pathos but of melancholia. With the humor, the craftsmanship and the action there was often, besides, a fine, still and sometimes dreamlike beauty. Much of his Civil War picture *The General* is within hailing distance of Mathew Brady. And there is a ghostly, unforgettable moment in *The Navigator* when, on a deserted, softly rolling ship, all the pale doors along a deck swing open as one behind Keaton and, as one, slam shut, in a hair-raising illusion of noise.

Perhaps because "dry" comedy is so much more rare and odd than "dry" wit, there are people who never much cared for Keaton. Those who do cannot care mildly.

As soon as the screen began to talk, silent comedy was pretty well finished. The hardy and prolific Mack Sennett made the transfer; he was the first man to put Bing Crosby and W.C. Fields on the screen. But he was essentially a silent-picture man, and by the time the Academy awarded him a special Oscar for his "lasting contribution to the comedy technique of the screen" (in 1938), he was no longer active. As for the comedians we have spoken of in particular, they were as badly off as fine dancers suddenly required to appear in plays.

Harold Lloyd, whose work was most nearly realistic, naturally coped least unhappily with the added realism of speech; he made several talking comedies. But good as the best were, they were not so good as his silent work, and by the late thirties he quit acting. A few years ago he returned to play the lead (and play it beautifully) in Preston Sturges's *The Sin of Harold Diddlebock,* but this exceptional picture—which opened, brilliantly, with the closing reel of Lloyd's *The Freshman*—has not yet been generally released.

Like Chaplin, Lloyd was careful of his money; he is still rich and active. Last June, in the presence of President Truman, he became Imperial Potentate of the A.A.O.N.M.S. (Shriners). Harry Langdon, as we have said, was a broken man when sound came in.

Up to the middle thirties Buster Keaton made several feature-length pictures (with such players as Jimmy Durante, Wallace Beery and Robert Montgomery); he also made a couple of dozen talking shorts. Now and again he managed to get loose into motion, without having to talk, and for a moment or so the screen would start singing again. But his dark, dead voice, though it was in keeping with the visual character, tore his intensely silent style to bits and destroyed the illusion within which he worked. He gallantly and correctly refuses to regard himself as "retired." Besides occasional bits, spots and minor roles in Hollywood pictures, he has worked on summer stages, made talking comedies in France and Mexico and clowned in a French circus. This summer he has played the straw hats in *Three Men on a Horse.* He is planning a television program. He also has a working agreement with Metro. One of his jobs there is to construct comedy sequences for Red Skelton.

The only man who really survived the flood was Chaplin, the only one who was rich, proud and popular enough to afford to stay silent. He brought out two of his greatest nontalking comedies, *City Lights* and *Modern Times,* in the middle of an avalanche of talk, spoke gibberish and, in the closing moments, plain English in *The Great Dictator,* and at last made an all talking picture, *Monsieur Verdoux,* creating for that purpose an entirely new character who might properly talk a blue streak. *Verdoux* is the greatest of talking comedies though so cold and savage that it had to find its public in grimly experienced Europe.

Good comedy, and some that was better than good, outlived silence, but there has been less and less of it. The talkies brought one great comedian, the late, majestically lethargic W.C. Fields, who could not possibly have worked as well in silence; he was the toughest and the most warmly human of all screen comedians, and *It's A Gift* and *The Bank Dick,* fiendishly funny and incisive white-collar comedies, rank high among the best comedies (and best movies) ever made. Laurel and Hardy, the only comedians who managed to preserve much of the large, low style of silence and who began to explore the comedy of sound, have made nothing since 1945. Walt Disney, at his best an inspired comic inventor and teller of fairy stories, lost his stride during the war and has since regained it only at moments. Preston Sturges has made brilliant, satirical comedies, but his pictures are smart, nervous comedy-dramas merely italicized with slapstick. The Marx Brothers were side-splitters but they made their best comedies years ago. Jimmy Durante is mainly a nightclub genius; Abbot and Costello are semiskilled laborers, at best; Bob Hope is a good radio comedian with a pleasing presence, but not much more, on the screen.

There is no hope that screen comedy will get much better than it is without new, gifted young comedians who really belong in movies, and without freedom for their experiments. For everyone who may appear we have one last, invidious comparison to offer as a guidepost.

One of the most popular more recent comedies is Bob Hope's *The Paleface.* We take no pleasure in blackening *The Paleface;* we single it out, rather, because it is as good as we've got. Anything that is said of it here could be said, with interest, of other comedies of our time. Most of the laughs in *The Paleface* are verbal. Bob Hope is very adroit with his lines and now and then, when the words don't get in the way, he makes a good beginning as a visual comedian. But only the beginning, never the middle or the end. He is funny, for instance, reacting to a shot of violent whisky. But he does not know how to get still funnier (*i.e.,* how to build and milk) or how to be funniest last (*i.e.,* how to top or cap his gag). The camera has to fade out on the same old face he started with.

One sequence is promisingly set up for visual comedy. In it, Hope and a lethal local boy stalk each other all over a cow town through streets which have been emptied in fear of their duel. The gag here is that through accident and stupidity they keep just failing to find each other. Some of it is quite funny. But the fun slackens between laughs like a weak clothesline, and by all the logic of humor (which is ruthlessly logical) the biggest laugh should come at the moment, and through the way, they finally spot each other. The sequence is so weakly thought out that at that crucial moment the camera can't afford to watch them; it switches to Jane Russell.

Now we turn to a masterpiece. In *The Navigator* Buster Keaton works with practically the same gag as Hope's duel. Adrift on a ship which he believes is otherwise empty, he drops a lighted cigarette. A girl finds it. She calls out and he hears her; each then tries to find the other. First each walks purposefully down the long, vacant starboard deck, the girl, then Keaton, turning the corner just in time not to see each other. Next time around each of them is trotting briskly, very much in earnest; going at the same pace, they miss each other just the same. Next time around each of them is going like a bat out of hell. Again they miss. Then the camera withdraws to a point of vantage at the stern, leans its chin in its hand and just watches the whole intricate superstructure of the ship as the protagonists stroll, steal and scuttle from level to level, up, down and sidewise, always managing to miss each other by hair's-breadths, in an enchantingly neat and elaborate piece of timing. There are no subsidiary gags to get laughs in this sequence and there is little loud laughter; merely a quiet and steadily increasing kind of delight. When Keaton has got all he can out of this fine modification of the movie chase he invents a fine device to bring the two together: the girl, thoroughly winded, sits down for a breather, indoors, on a plank which workmen have left across sawhorses. Keaton pauses on an upper deck, equally winded and puzzled. What follows happens in a couple of seconds at most: air suction whips his silk topper backward down a ventilator; grabbing frantically for it, he backs against the lip of the ventilator, jacknifes and falls in backward. Instantly the camera cuts back to the girl. A topper falls through the ceiling and lands tidily, right side up, on the plank beside her. Before she can look more than startled, its owner follows, head between his knees, crushes the topper, breaks the plank with the point of his spine and proceeds to the floor. The breaking of the plank smacks Boy and Girl together.

It is only fair to remember that the silent comedians would have as hard a time playing a talking scene as Hope has playing his visual ones, and that writing and directing are as accountable for the failure as Hope himself. But not even the humblest journeymen of the silent years would have let themselves off so easily. Like the masters, they knew, and sweated to obey, the laws of their craft.

Ben Turpin in *The Shriek of Araby*

Playing the Dozens

"Playing the dozens" is part of the language of the black ghetto. It is a verbal contest in which the players strive to top each other with insults. By successfully playing the dozens, a person can establish his personality and control people and situations in order to give himself a winning edge.

● ● ● ● ●

I'm so broke, I couldn't buy a crippled crab a crutch if I had a forest of small trees.

Yeah, well I'm so broke, I couldn't buy a mosquito a wrestling jacket, and that's a small fit.

My soles are so thin that if I stepped on a dime I could tell whether it's heads or tails.

I'm so hungry my backbone is almost shaking hands with
my stomach.

I'm so hungry I could see a bow-legged biscuit walk a crooked
mile.

You look like death standing on a street corner
eating lifesavers.

I'm so broke, if they were selling Philadelphia for a penny,
I'd have to run, afraid they would sell it to the wrong person.

Your house is so small, the roaches have to walk sideways
through the hallways.

Man, you're so dark, you need a license to drink white milk.

SMASHED POTATOES: A KID'S-EYE VIEW OF THE KITCHEN

Jane G. Martel

A WHOLE TURKEY

1 big bag full of a whole turkey (Get the kind with no feathers on—not the kind the Pilgrims ate.)

A giant lump of stuffin'

1 squash pie

1 mint pie

1 little fancy dish of sour berries

1 big fancy dish of a vegetable mix

20 dishes of all different candies; chocolate balls, cherry balls, good'n plenties and peanuts

Get up when the alarm says to and get busy fast. Unfold the turkey and open up the holes. Push in the stuffin' for a couple hours. I think you get stuffin' from that Farm that makes it.

I know you have to pin the stuffin' to the turkey or I suppose it would get out. And get special pins or use big long nails.

Get the kitchen real hot, and from there on you just cook turkey. Sometimes you can call it a bird, but it's not.

Then you put the vegetables in the cooker—and first put one on top, and next put one on the bottom, and then one in the middle. That makes a vegetable mix. Put 2 red things of salt all in it and 2 red things of water also. Cook them to just ½ of warm.

Put candies all around the place and Linda will bring over the pies.

When the company comes put on your red apron.

BASKETTI

with macaronis and noodles

1 whole pack of long sticks—get them the size you want them.
Orangey-red spicy stuff for topping (2 little kinds and 2 big kinds)
1 half of a quarter of water
Many purple onions with the paper off
Use red meat balls and the soapy kind of cheese that tastes a little bit
    rotten.

For the cooking get a stove, and pots, and bowls, and spoons and gloves
with pink flowers.

Cook for quite a while.

The only thing is—when you have it, your father has to stay home for
the day because he takes the basketti out of the pan and squeezes out
the water.

Serves all 4 of us—but not Freddy.

CHOPS

Some chops that are enough to fill up your pan
Fresh salt and pepper
Fresh flour
1 ball of salad lettuce
1 sponge cake with ice cream

Put the chops in the bag and shake them for 5 hours—and the flour too.

Put them in a skillet pan on the biggest black circle on the roof of
your stove. Cook them for plenty of time.

Fringe up the lettuce in little heaps in all the bowls.

Go on the porch and bring the high chair and have your supper
everybody!

Note: But stoves really are dangerous—and you shouldn't go near
one till you get married.

PLAIN NOODLES

'cause they're my best

1 little triangle of butter this big
1 whole thing of noodles
An amount of salt
The same of pepper
Whatever else you need

Take the thing with high edges (not exactly a pan) and put 10 pounds of boiling water in it. Put the noodles in for I wouldn't guess how long. Your mother knows because she can tell time. One thing for sure —when you touch them they feel slippery-wet.

I suppose you could have other stuff with it if you want . . .

And some people have milk to drink and some have martinis.

CHINESE FOOD

6 bones
2 sauce
20 inches of Chinese rice
1 basket of chowmeins
1 basket of Kung foo yung
6 tan cookies with paper inside

Warm it all good and hot while you bake it by the stove. Put the sauce on the bones. When they get red they are through with the baking.

Put the baskets on the table, and the rice and the red bones.

Eat it for dinner and leave the rest for leftovers. Then it is time to open up the cookies and read them.

It makes a Chinese dinner for 3 people. But all kinds of people can eat it. You don't have to be Chinese.

BANILLA CAKE

1 cake stuff
2 eggs (But on "Sesame Street" they put 8 eggs in a cake. I always
   watch "Love American Style" after "Sesame Street.")
A drop of milk
7 of those little silver baseballs for on the top.

Put every single thing you have into a mother-size pan—a little one
wouldn't do.

Put it in the oven department of the stove. Make it as hot as a coffee
pot.

Pretty soon it will come popping right out!

Eat it when the news comes on.

"first you open the eggs with your mittens"

ACKNOWLEDGMENTS

Charles Addams: For cartoon from *Nightcrawlers* by Charles Addams. Thomas Y. Crowell Company: For world rights for "Plane Geometry" by Emma Round from *Imagination's Other Place* by Helen Plotz; copyright 1955 by Thomas Y. Crowell Company, Inc. Gerald Duckworth & Company Ltd.: For British Commonwealth rights for "Resume" and "Coda" by Dorothy Parker from *The Collected Dorothy Parker*. Doubleday & Company, Inc.: For world rights for "The Ransom of Red Chief" from *Whirligigs* by O. Henry; copyright 1907 by Doubleday & Company, Inc. J. M. Dent & Sons Ltd.: For rights for the British Empire excluding Canada for "The Turtle," "The Fish," "The Rabbits," "The Germ," "The Rhinoceros," and "The Cow" by Ogden Nash from *Verses from 1929 On*. For "The Shrew," "The Stork," and "The Pigeon" by Ogden Nash from *The Face Is Familiar*. E.C. Publications: For "Jabberwhacky Or on Dreaming after Falling Asleep Watching TV" by Isabelle Di Caprio from *Mad Magazine*; copyright © 1963 by E.C. Publications, Inc. For material from *Mad Special Number Six*; © 1971 by E.C. Publications, Inc. Grosset & Dunlap, Inc.: For world rights for "Comedy's Greatest Era" from *Agee on Film: Vol. I* by James Agee; copyright © 1958 by The James Agee Trust. Harper & Row Publishers, Inc.: For world rights for "Christmas Afternoon" by Robert Benchley from *The Benchley Roundup*, selected by Nathaniel Benchley; copyright 1921 by Harper & Row Publishers, Inc. For world rights for "Happy Childhood Tales" by Robert Benchley from *The Benchley Roundup*, selected by Nathaniel Benchley; copyright 1932 by Robert C. Benchley. For world rights for "At the Funeral" and "At a Fire" from *Letters from the Earth* by Mark Twain, edited by Bernard DeVoto; copyright © 1962 by The Mark Twain Company. For world rights for "The Late Benjamin Franklin" and "A Fine Old Man" from *Sketches New and Old* by Mark Twain. For world rights for "A Page from a Californian Almanac" from *The Celebrated Jumping Frog of Calaveras County and Other Sketches* by Mark Twain. For use of the Mark Twain registered trademark. Hamish Hamilton, London: For British Commonwealth rights for drawing from *Vintage Thurber* by James Thurber; copyright © 1963 by Helen Thurber. For British Commonwealth rights except Canada for "The Secret Life of Walter Mitty" from *Vintage Thurber*; copyright © 1963 by Hamish Hamilton. Houghton Mifflin Company: For world rights for material from *Smashed Potatoes: A Kid's Eye View of the Kitchen* by Jane G. Martel; copyright © 1974 by Jane G. Martel. International Famous Agency and Art Buchwald: For British Commonwealth rights for "The Grown-Up Problem" from *Son of the Great Society* by Art Buchwald. Little, Brown and Company: For "The Turtle" and "The Fish" from *Verses from 1929 On* by Ogden Nash; copyright 1940. For "The Rabbits" and "The Cow" from *Verses from 1929 On* by Ogden Nash; copyright 1931. For "The Germ" from *Verses from 1929 On* by Ogden Nash; copyright 1935 by The Curtis Publishing Company. For "The Rhinoceros" from *Verses from 1929 On* by Ogden Nash; copyright 1933 by Ogden Nash; originally appeared in *The New Yorker*. For "The Shrew" from *The Face Is Familiar* by Ogden Nash; copyright 1940 by The Curtis Publishing Company. For "The Pigeon" from *The Face Is Familiar* by Ogden Nash; copyright 1940 by Ogden Nash. For "The Stork" by Ogden Nash; copyright 1933 by Ogden Nash. For cartoons; copyright 1973 by The New Yorker Magazine, Inc. MacDonald and Company Ltd.: For world rights for "Sleeping Arrangements" from *Everything but Money* by Sam Levenson. McGraw-Hill Book Company: For world rights for "The Discovery of America" from *It All Started with Columbus* by Richard Armour; copyright © 1961 by Richard Armour. G. P. Putnam's Sons: For "The Grown-up Problem" from *Son of the Great Society* by Art Buchwald; copyright © 1965, 1966 by Art Buchwald. William Saroyan: For "Fable IX" from *Saroyan's Fables*. Simon & Schuster, Inc.: For "Sleeping Arrangements" from *Everything but Money* by Sam Levenson; copyright © 1949, 1951, 1952, 1953, 1955, 1956, 1958, 1961, 1966 by Sam Levenson. Mrs. James Thurber: For "The Secret Life of Walter Mitty" from *My World—And Welcome to It* by James Thurber, published by Harcourt Brace Jovanovich, originally printed in *The New Yorker*; copyright © 1942 by James Thurber; copyright © 1970 by Helen Thurber. For "A New Natural History" from *The Beast in Me—And Other Animals* by James Thurber, published by Harcourt Brace Jovanovich, New York, originally printed in *The New Yorker*; copyright © 1948 by James Thurber. Triangle Publications, Inc. and Bonnie O'Boyle: For "Graffiti Lives" by Bonnie O'Boyle, reprinted from *Seventeen;* copyright © 1969 by Triangle Publications, Inc. The Viking Press: For "Resume" from *The Portable Dorothy Parker*; copyright 1926, 1954 by Dorothy Parker. For "Coda" from *The Portable Dorothy Parker*; copyright 1928, © 1956 by Dorothy Parker.

ILLUSTRATION